HOPE RENEWED

THROUGH EYES OF FAITH

I pray that the eyes of your heart may be
enlightened in order that you may know
the hope to which he has called you...

~ Ephesians 1:18

Idella Pearl Edwards

FRONT COVER PHOTO: Granddaughter, Christine Andersen

BACK COVER PHOTO: By Janet Bixler, Eldorado, IL

This is a revised edition of "HOPE Through Eyes of Faith"

Dedicated
to
Every man, woman and child
Who has ever struggled
With a loss of hope

Shawnee National Forest, Photo by Jim Martin

Hope is like the sun, which, as we journey towards it, casts the shadow of our burden behind us. Hope sweetens the memory of experiences well loved. It tempers our troubles to our growth and our strength.

It befriends us in the dark hours, excites us in bright ones. It lends promise to the future and purpose to the past. It turns discouragement to determination.

~ Samuel Smiles (1812-1904)

CONTENTS

We have this hope
as an anchor for the soul,
firm and secure.

~ Hebrews 6:19

What gives me the most hope
every day is God's grace;
knowing that his grace is going
to give me the strength
for whatever I face,
knowing that nothing
is a surprise to God.

~ Rick Warren

FOREWORD

A wise Christian teacher once observed: *"The real challenge of Christianity is its dailyness!"* No wonder Jesus taught us to pray for *daily* bread. It is in our daily living that we show best *"we are not like others in the world; we are people of hope."*

Former church member, Idella Pearl Edwards, has given us the perfect companion for our daily journey of faith: a little book entitled HOPE RENEWED. Here, you will find over 85 lively devotions that combine scripture, stories, poetry and photography to "jumpstart" any day with positive and hope-filled thoughts.

Like Jesus, the master story-teller, Idella's stories are filled with humor, family and faith: a cat named Bamm-Bamm, a berry-picking bear, the vicious bite of "no-see-ums," a play-dough cookie prank . . . And then for personal application, thought-provoking questions at the end called PONDERINGS, followed by a closing thought from a person of history or quote from Scripture. Altogether well-constructed, delightfully ordinary and yet spiritually uplifting. I heartily recommend HOPE RENEWED.

~ Dr. Stan Cosby
Saint Stephen United Methodist Church
Amarillo, Texas

Stan Cosby is a sixth generation Methodist, a descendant of circuit riding preachers. He was born March 20, 1952 to Betty and Olin Cosby in Canyon, Texas. He and his wife, Susan, have three children, nine grandchildren and one great-grandchild. Stan has a Bachelor of Arts degree (cum laude) from McMurry University, a Master of Divinity degree from Asbury Theological Seminary and a Doctor of Ministry degree from Oral Roberts University. He has ministered in India, Russia, Ghana, Mexico, Peru, Lebanon, Nigeria, Malawi, Thailand, Sri Lanka, Guatemala and Kenya. A true evangelist at heart, there is nothing Stan would rather do than share the love of Jesus Christ with others.

1

hope

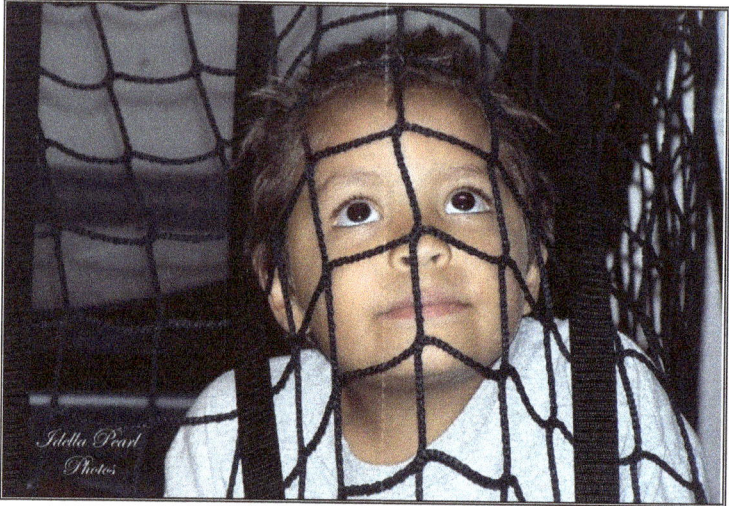

Grandson, David Andersen

Christian hope makes us have
that confidence in God,
in his ultimate triumph,
and in his goodness and love,
which nothing can shake.

~ Eli Stanley Jones (1884-1973)

INTRODUCTION

Dear Readers,

"HOPE RENEWED" is a revision of my book, "HOPE, Through Eyes of Faith." I decided to rewrite it for two reasons:

1) I felt each devotional needed a color photo to represent the subject and to cement the spiritual applications into our hearts and minds. Adults, as well as children, need visual stimulation. Hopefully, the pictures will add a delightful dimension that will encourage us, inspire us, and give us a vision of all that we were meant to accomplish as disciples of Jesus Christ.

2) The previous book was written specifically for dieters and as such, spoke to a limited audience. I am praying that the rewrite will give the book a universal appeal and help illumine the pathway of those who find themselves in dark places. Hopefully it will assist all of us to rediscover the joy of serving Jesus. I have kept the original stories, but have altered some of the applications to meet a wider variety of spiritual needs.

Thank you for choosing to read this book! I pray God will speak to your heart and that you will receive a blessing and a renewed hope in the future.

LET'S BEGIN OUR JOURNEY TOGETHER

Each of us reading this book would love to look into the future and see ourselves doing a victory dance. Before the hope of the future can become a reality however, we must first look to the past.

One of the saints of the past that has influenced my life is E. Stanley Jones. Jones' life was greatly changed during a revival on the campus of Asbury College in Wilmore, Kentucky. He said the

Holy Spirit liberated him from a sense of superiority. He was considered to be the "Billy Graham" of India where he served as a missionary for over sixty years. E. Stanley Jones started a movement of spiritual retreats called United Christian Ashrams. My husband and I were on the Board of Directors for the Oklahoma United Christian Ashram for several years. In the early 1970's, we were privileged to hear Jones preach in Chillicothe, Ohio.

E. Stanley Jones has been an inspiration to thousands. He was a pure example of loving the Lord with heart, soul, strength and mind and his neighbor as himself. I have included a few of his spirit-filled prayers in some of the devotionals.

The saints of the past can be stepping-stones to victory as we imitate their faith and faithfulness. There are many saints we can admire from Biblical times and throughout history.

Another saint of the past who has greatly influenced my life is my mother, Esther Edwards. (Yes, her married name is the same as my married name.) She passed away at the age of 100. During her lifetime, she consistently looked for ways in which her life could be a blessing to others. For years, she played the piano for the Senior Center and even played a piano concert at her own 100th Birthday party, a portion of which can be seen at:

https://www.youtube.com/watch?v=1QzfgngzQkg

She was the valedictorian of her high school class in Whitehall, Wisconsin in 1925. In her speech she spoke about the River of Life: *"Let us hope that each one of us will steer his boat well and that the Great River of Humanity may flow on more smoothly, with a deeper, happier song, because we have become a part of it."*

My mother wrote the following poem at the age of 91. It reflects her generosity of spirit and a belief that each day of her life was precious.

TODAY

In the early morning it began,
A day that will never return again.
We fill the hours with work and play
And believe we've had a pretty good day.

But then today becomes the past,
When tomorrow comes at last.
We look back and try to recall
If we had done any good at all.

Did we help anybody along the way?
Did we say, "I love you" or think to pray?
Did we teach our children right from wrong?
Did we brighten our day as we sang a song?

Now we come to the end of another day
And tomorrow will become
Another today.

~ Esther Edwards

My mother lived the last 28 years of her life in our home. Her beliefs were clear, and they did not vary from what she practiced. God desires that our lives, as well, be a blessing to others, both physically and spiritually.

There is not one day of our lives of which we can say, *"It's not that important. I always have tomorrow."* Each day is a precious gift to be lived to the glory of God! May God help us so that apathy and forgetfulness do not steal our resolve and consume our victory. Come with me as we begin a spiritual journey that will make a difference. May your hope become reality!

Blessings,
Idella

So here's what I want you to do,
God helping you:
Take your everyday, ordinary life –
your sleeping, eating, going-to-work,
and walking-around life –
and place it before God as an offering.
Embracing what God does for you
is the best thing you can do for him.

Romans 12:1 (MSG)

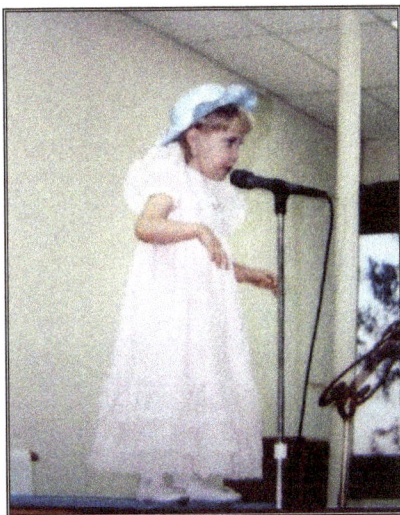
Granddaughter, Jackie Edwards

EEEWWW, WHAT A MESS!

One of my favorite memories is of our three-year-old granddaughter, Jackie, singing a solo for the Annual Talent Show at Green Valley United Methodist Church in Henderson, Nevada. The song began with, *"I'm bringing home a baby bumblebee. Won't my mommy be so proud of me!"* The song told of the bee stinging her and how she squished it with her hands and wiped it on her dress. The next line in the song, which Jackie performed with the great drama of a 3-year-old, was, *"Eeewww, what a mess!"*

I had my own mess one time when I opened my purse to retrieve a ballpoint pen. We had been to McDonald's that day with our grandchildren, David and Christine. When cleaning up the table, I grabbed what I thought to be an unopened package of caramel sauce the grandkids had not used for their apple dippers and threw it into my purse. Evidently it HAD been opened. *"Eeewww, what a mess!"*

Sadly, there are those of us who can look at our lives and say the same thing, *"Eeewww, what a mess!"* Our finances are out of control, our relationships are a mess, our bad habits far outnumber our good ones, our emotions are frazzled and our spiritual life is bedraggled.

There are consequences for messes. The little girl in Jackie's song received consequences from her mommy for soiling her pretty dress. Jackie dramatically ended her song with, *"Ouch! She spanked me!"* The messes in our lives each have their own consequences. Some messes might be avoided or resolved by using a little wisdom and/or diligence. If I had thought to check the seal on the caramel sauce before I threw it into my purse, I could have avoided the goo, but I was able to clean it up with a little diligence. Other messes in our lives are not as easy to clean. In fact, no matter how hard we try, the stains remain.

When we take a long, hard look at our lives, sometimes the only thing we can honestly say is, *"Eeewww, what a mess!"* These types of messes do not clean up easily. Perhaps it's time to find a power cleaner. Max Lucado tells us that: *"Conversion is more than a removal of sin. It's a deposit of power!"* That power is found only in the precious blood of Jesus. No matter how hard we try to use our own elbow grease to scrub away the grime of our rebellious nature, the dirt and stain will remain. But when we bring the mess to Jesus, 1 John 1:7 tells us that, *"...the blood of Jesus, (God's) Son, purifies us from all sin."*

PONDERINGS

~ Which area of your life is the messiest? What happened?

~ Read 1 Kings 4:29 and 1 Kings 11:4. How could someone so wise make such a mess of life?

~ Why is it so tempting to sweep our mess under the rug rather than allow Jesus to clean it up?

O God, purify each heart with refining fire, let perfect love in us abound. With all dross removed and each vain desire; O Father, send the power down. Amen.
~ Lyrics by Ella V. Phillips (1987 Public Domain)

Granddaughters, Meghan and Colleen Malone

HOW MUCH IS ENOUGH?

How much is enough? How much of any one thing do we need to make us happy? If something makes us happy, will a larger amount of the same thing make us even happier? It sounds logical but it doesn't always work that way. Many of the things that bring us joy also have the capability, in excess quantities, of stealing that same joy. Even the good things in life have limits.

1) Pets are good, providing companionship and love, but it might get a little expensive to feed 18 dogs and 23 cats. 2) Medicine is good, but too much medicine could cause problems worse than the original sickness. 3) Sunshine is good, but after living for three years in the Mohave Desert, my skin cried out for a little moisture. 4) Rain is good, but after spending three years living on a river in West Virginia that flooded twice a year, I would have preferred a little less moisture. 5) A nice breeze is good, especially on a hot summer day, but after living in Tornado Alley for 14 years (also known as Oklahoma City) we would have preferred a little less wind. 6) Love is good, but if we hold hands all day it will be difficult to tie our shoelaces. 7) Food is good but too much can raise havoc with our health, our self-esteem and our relationships.

9

How much is enough? It's hard to imagine getting too much of a good thing, but it can happen. We lived in Oklahoma City at the time of the 1995 Murrah Federal Building bombing. When rescue workers ran out of supplies, the need was advertised on television. Within an hour, a new announcement was made to stop sending supplies. The response had been so great that it created an overabundance, and the cars attempting delivery were lined up for blocks, hampering rescue efforts.

Even good things have limits. How much does it take before we are satisfied? If we are trying to satisfy all our spiritual needs with the things of this world, they will NEVER be enough. Isaiah 55:2 gives us wise advice: *"Why spend money on what is not bread, and your labor on what does not satisfy? Listen, listen to me, and eat what is good, and you will delight in the richest of fare."*

How much is enough? When we know beyond a shadow of doubt that God is enough, our contentment will never be contingent upon the things of this world.

PONDERINGS

~ What is the difference between satisfaction and pleasure? What gives you the most contentment?

~ What things do we turn to for satisfaction that really don't satisfy?

~ Was there a time when you felt like giving up? What was the last straw? Maude Royden (1876-1956) said, *"When you have nothing left but God, you will realize God is enough."* What makes this attitude possible?

O Almighty God! Eternal Treasury of all good things! Let your Providence be my storehouse, my own necessities the measure of my desire. Amen.   ~ Jeremy Taylor (1613-1667)

Blessings

May you have enough.....

Enough happiness to keep you sweet,
Enough trials to keep you strong,
Enough sorrow to keep you human,
Enough failure to keep you humble,
Enough success to keep you eager,
Enough friends to give you comfort,
Enough wealth to meet your needs,
Enough enthusiasm to look forward,
Enough faith to banish depression,
Enough determination to make each day
  better than yesterday.

May you have enough.

~ Source unknown

Bruce Edwards' Lake Superior Agate

My hope is built on nothing less
Than Jesus' blood and righteousness;
I dare not trust the sweetest frame,
But wholly lean on Jesus' name.

Refrain:

On Christ, the solid Rock, I stand;
All other ground is sinking sand,
All other ground is sinking sand.

When darkness veils His lovely face,
I rest on His unchanging grace;
In every high and stormy gale,
My anchor holds within the veil.

Edward Mote (1797-1874)

12

Lake Michigan Stones
Photo by Kim Vanderhelm

SOLID AS A ROCK

I love stones – not rough ordinary gray rocks, but smooth polished stones with interesting patterns and colors. Our family spent many hours on Lake Superior searching for agates. An agate is a semi-precious gemstone with eye-catching banding patterns that formed millions of years ago.

The best time to find agates is usually after a storm when the waves have churned up the rocks and tumbled them toward shore. Agates are easier to spot when they are wet so we would wade barefooted into the water and search until our feet turned blue from the cold. We were usually rewarded for our efforts with some beautiful agates.

One Ash Wednesday at church, we were asked to pick out one stone from a large bowl of stones. They were not agates, but I was intrigued with the beautiful colors. I took my time, choosing an unusual and attractive stone. It was jet black, smooth to the touch and filled with variegated gray stripes.

At the end of the service, we were invited to spend some time thinking about the stone each of us had chosen and what sin it represented. Then we were to place our stone into a large bowl of water representing The Sea of God's Forgiveness. By that time I was becoming attached to my pretty little stone but, because the stone represented my sin, I knew I had to give it up. Our pastor, Rev. Tim Ozment, encouraged us by saying: *"That stone has no life of its own - only the life we give it."*

Our sin is like a pretty stone. It looks harmless enough...it's intriguing to look at...it seems comforting to caress the smooth surface, and the longer we hold it close, it becomes like an old friend. But it makes no sense to trust in the pebbles of life that churn and tumble about with each crashing wave.

God is asking us to give up our fascination for the colorful pebbles of life and fix our gaze on the magnetic, flawless beauty of Jesus, our Solid Rock. God is asking us to place our trust in the unshakable foundation of his mercy, love and care.

"The LORD is my rock, my fortress and my deliverer; my God is my rock, in whom I take refuge, my shield and the horn of my salvation, my stronghold." (Psalm 18:2)

PONDERINGS

~ Read James 5:16. What benefit might there be in confessing our sins to one another? Is it always necessary?

~ Which sin am I most attached to? What excuses do I use for not giving it up?

~ Why is the word "rock" a good description for Jesus? How is Jesus a Rock for me?

Lord, wearied by the conflicts of life, worn by the burdens of the day, we seek You as our resting place. May Your eternal calm descend upon our troubled spirits and give us Your peace. Amid the treacherous sands of time, You stand still, the Rock of Ages! Amen.   ~ W. E. Orchard (1877-1955)

14

Bamm-Bamm

EVERY LITTER BIT

I "cat-sat" a while back for the four cats belonging to my daughter and son-in-law, Rhonda and Jim. Bamm-Bamm, a large, gray, lazy cat, required insulin shots. He was an easy cat to care for because of his laid-back personality and friendliness. I didn't have to search for him. I just called, *"Bamm-Bamm, insulin! Bamm-Bamm, kitty treat!"* He would come sauntering up and wait for me to perform my task and give him a kitty treat.

I liked giving the insulin shot to Bamm-Bamm better than I liked cleaning the litter boxes. With Bamm-Bamm, Sam, Zoey and Grimmy, there was a lot of, shall we say, accumulation. I pulled my turtleneck shirt up over my nose and used the scoop to dig in and empty out. Sometimes we don't like to do the things we have to do. Although I don't like cleaning litter boxes, I also don't like the idea of the cats having to use a litter box that is not clean. The choice is clear.

We make choices every day. I may not want to do the dishes, but if I want to eat on a clean plate, I will do something about it. I may not want to spend time reading my Bible, but if I want to know the truth and know the peace that comes from the love of God, I have to meditate on His Word. The choice is clear. But if the right choices are so clear, why do we sometimes make the wrong ones? It may have something to do with our stubborn nature. We want to do what WE want to do. The scripture in Psalm 32:9 may be speaking to some of us: *"Do not be like the horse or the mule, which have no understanding but must be controlled by bit and bridle or they will not come to you."*

Our son, David, came to live with us at the age of eleven from a children's home in Ohio. To put it mildly, he was quite a handful. If I scolded him for eating candy before dinner and the next night I had to scold him again for eating cookies before dinner, he would be indignant, responding with, *"But you told me not to eat candy before dinner. You never told me not to eat cookies."* It really didn't matter what the rule was - David had a rebel spirit.

We are all, on occasion, rebels. It may be time for us to dig in and empty out "every litter bit" of the rebellious attitudes that so easily influence our decisions. This will give us a fresh opportunity to experience all the wonderful things God has for us.

PONDERINGS

~ Were you rebellious as a teen? Compliant? Or somewhere in between?

~ Read John 14:15. What does love have to do with keeping God's commands?

~ Is rebellion always bad? What did David G. Wells mean when he said: *"Prayer is in essence rebellion - rebellion against the world in its fallenness."*

Have mercy upon me, O God, according to Your lovingkindness; according to the multitude of Your tender mercies, blot out my transgressions. Create in me a clean heart, O God, and renew a steadfast spirit within me. Amen. (Psalm 51:1, 10 NKJV)

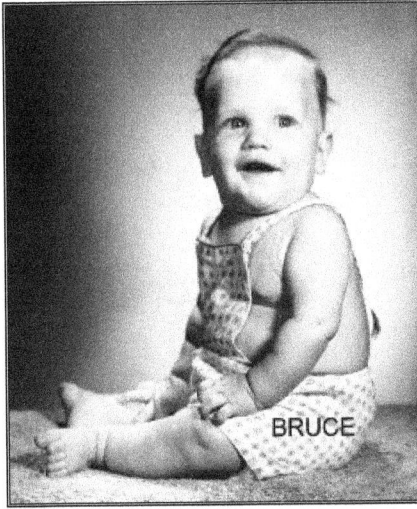

BRUCE

ARMS OF LOVE

When our son Bruce was a small baby, I didn't get much done. It was not because I was overwhelmed with the new responsibilities of motherhood, but rather that I was fascinated with this new little life. This tiny bundle, so warm and so soft, was my gift from God. I loved to sit and watch him by the hour, filled with the wonder that I was now a 21-year-old mother and this beautiful child was mine.

One glorious spring morning, I opened all the windows. The sun was streaming in, so I laid Bruce on a soft blanket on the carpet in the living room. I lay beside him while he slept just watching him breathe and studying every tiny miracle of fingers and toes. I left for a moment to get a second cup of coffee from the kitchen.

When I returned, I was horrified to see an enormous army of ants marching steadily forward across the carpet from a nearby window toward my 3-month-old child. I ran and swept him up into my arms, snuggling him close to my heart while I retrieved the vacuum cleaner from the hall closet and began frantically sucking up ants from the carpet. I was like a mama bear fiercely protecting her baby cub. I still remember the adrenaline rush and my dogged

17

determination that I would let absolutely nothing harm this precious child whom I loved with heart and soul.

I love the story in the Bible that tells how much Jesus longed to sweep His children up in His arms. *"O Jerusalem, Jerusalem, you who kill the prophets and stone those sent to you, how often I have longed to gather your children together, as a hen gathers her chicks under her wings, but you were not willing."* (Matthew 23:37)

The "heart and soul" kind of love mothers have for their children is merely a reflection of the enormous love God has for His children. We don't always know how much God protects us because we, like an infant, are oblivious to the dangers around us. (Of course, some of the ants marching our way are following a long trail of the crumbs of self-indulgence.) But our God knows our weaknesses and stands ready to rescue us from the evil one.

Christians have no fear of Satan's open windows because we know that Satan cannot touch a hair on our head without God's permission. We are blessed because God *"...has rescued us from the dominion of darkness and brought us into the kingdom of the Son he loves."* (Colossians 1:13)

PONDERINGS

~ Read Zephaniah 3:17. What are the similarities between a mother's love and God's love?

~ What are you afraid of? What fears could you get rid of if you were convinced that God was always close, watching over you?

~ There's an expression, *"Feed your faith and your doubts will starve to death."* How do we put this into practice?

O God, hold me fast and let no power of the enemy take me out of Your hand; let nothing anymore divide me from You. Amen.
~ Household Prayers (1864)

PLAYING WITH FIRE

As a child, I had a great deal of freedom. In the 1940's, it was a safer world in which to live, and parents didn't have to hold the reins as tightly. Also, my mother worked full time and could not afford a babysitter during the summer or after school. My father was an alcoholic, and mother worked long hours to put bread on the table. She depended on the neighbors to keep an eye on me.

I enjoyed my summers. It was a time to experiment and explore. When I was seven years old, my ten-year-old brother, Bobby, used to take me with him to play on the railroad tracks. When a train stopped, we climbed up one of those "fun" ladders on the side of a car, waited until the train started to go and then dared each other to be the last one to jump off and roll. If the conductor saw us, he yelled at us about the dangers, but we would just laugh and run away. After all, we never got hurt. How could it be dangerous?

In the fall after school, we had fun building large bonfires out of fallen leaves. My brother and his friends dared each other to run and jump over the fire. I was never that brave. Instead, my friends and I liked to "roast" potatoes by wrapping them in tinfoil, and burying them in the fire. When they were "done," we ate them voraciously and, although we convinced ourselves they were

19

delicious, they were always burnt on the outside, raw in the middle and tasted slightly like tin.

As an adult, I no longer play on railroad tracks nor do I play with fire. Fire can be useful when used for the purpose for which it was created but when used carelessly, it can become utterly destructive. The same is true of our spiritual lives. When we are careless about our attitudes, our actions or even our relationship with God, we will end up being burned. Although the Bible is clear on the consequences of complacency, we adopt a spirit of immunity. Surely, consequences only happen to others! We may gamble for a while and win, but eventually our poor decisions will backfire.

God stands ready to help us. 2 Timothy 1:7 says that the Spirit, *"...gives us power, love and self-discipline."* With God's help we can put out the flames of our self-seeking and begin to enjoy the blessings of a life in tune with a wise and loving God. Titus 2:12 tells us that God's grace, *"...teaches us to say 'No' to ungodliness and worldly passions, and to live self-controlled, upright and godly lives..."*

PONDERINGS

~ Did you ever play with fire as a child? What makes fire so fascinating? What makes sin so inviting?

~ Read Titus 2:11-12. What is the definition of grace? In what way is grace a "teacher"?

~ A few synonyms for "careless" are: haphazard, negligent, reckless, sloppy and thoughtless. What causes people to be careless about their spiritual life?

O God of comfort, hear our cry, and in the darkest hour draw nigh. Spare us, good Lord! If just the strife, yet still from guilt we are not free; forgive our blind and careless life, our oft forgetfulness of Thee. Amen.   ~ Lyrics from Hymns Ancient & Modern 1904

Costa Rica
Xinia, Jimi and Rhonda

WHEN IN ROME

We've all heard the expression, "When in Rome, do as the Romans do." If we are in a place where we are unfamiliar with the customs or traditions, we must be careful not to do or say anything that could be interpreted as offensive to the local people.

Our daughter, Rhonda, went on a mission trip to Costa Rica in 1986. During her two months there, she made a supreme effort to follow the customs of the local people. In a letter, she shared the following with us:

> It was quite a culture shock. The worse thing, worse than the four-inch cucarachas, worse than the hot sun and continuous sweat, worse than the cement taking layers of skin off my hands, worse than rice and beans three times a day, worse than the stomach issues we all had…is the smell by the baño (bathroom) and the smell outside our bedroom window. We have to go outside to get to the bathroom through the pigs and chickens. I'm pretty sure what we're smelling is the slaughtering. It's not all bad though…we're all in good spirits.
>
> I would patiently take a bug out of my rice and beans and keep eating. I shared my shower willingly with the spiders and

cockroaches and my bed with the fleas (flea bites are bad!) I patiently tossed and turned all night on the heat waves in time with the moos, oinks, cluck-clucks, cock-a-doodle-doos, bzzzs and ruffs. But I enjoyed myself! I really did.

There's a lot to appreciate. The people are super friendly and the church family loves the Lord immensely. I really am glad I came, and I'm having a wonderful and meaningful time!

Rhonda put aside her own personal comfort for what she considered to be the mission to which God had called her.

When in Rome, do as the Romans do. When in Costa Rica, do as the Costa Ricans do. We may not be in Rome nor in Costa Rica, but we are "in Christ." Our mission, should we choose to accept it, is to put aside our own personal agenda and follow the example of Jesus. Jesus said, *"I have set you an example that you should do as I have done for you."* (John 13:15) Therefore, "when in Christ," do as Christ would do!

PONDERINGS

~ Jesus' mission was to the whole person, both physical and spiritual. How important is a wholistic approach to missionary work?

~ Some believe that friendship evangelism requires Christians to become friends with unbelievers before telling them of their need for a Savior. Agree or disagree? Why?

~ How is the increased use of technology good for spreading the Gospel? How is it bad?

Lord, our God, bind us to all men and women of our time so that together we may bring the Good News to the ends of the earth. Open our hearts and our Christian communities to the needy, the afflicted, the oppressed. Amen.
~ The Propagation of the Faith Evangelization of the Nations

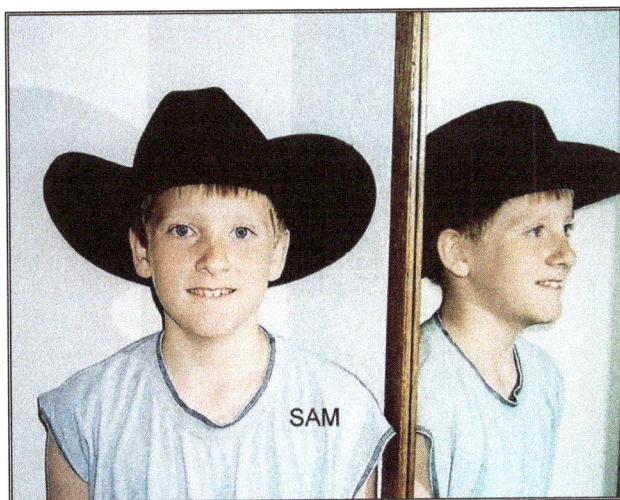
Grandson, Sam Edwards

ENCASED IN CEMENT

Our daughter, Kerry, enjoys reading articles describing, "What Kids Say About Love." One time, she decided to ask her nine-year-old son, Samuel, some pointed questions about love, even though he was "anti-girls."

- What is the proper age to get married?
  Sam: "100 – 'cause I want to die first."
- When is it okay to kiss someone?
  Sam: "Never - just 'cause. But you're supposed to ask first."
- What is falling in love like?
  Sam: "Bad, like when your cat scratches you in the eye."
- Confidential opinions about love.
  Sam: "My cat is soft and my rabbit is too. So I love them because they are soft and they aren't girls."
- Surefire ways to make a person fall in love with you.
  Sam: "If they ask, I'm gonna say NO…'cause a NO is a NO!"

Most nine-year-old boys have negative opinions about girls and love. They would rather have a tooth pulled than be seen with a girl! When Sam turned 16, I suspect he changed his mind regarding an opinion or two that were, at one time, "encased in cement." As we mature, or as facts are presented, we either change our minds or add more cement. If we continue adding layers of cement, it becomes increasingly difficult to change. We may grow fond of our cement or perhaps look at the thickness of the cement and become overwhelmed at the mere thought of change.

Where do we find the strength to change? God has generously given us two sources of power – His Holy Word and the Name of Jesus. *"For the word of God is living and powerful, and sharper than any two-edged sword..."* (Hebrews 4:12) *"...Most assuredly, I say to you, whatever you ask the Father in My name He will give you.."* (John 16:23 NKJV) Nothing works better for breaking up cement than His Word and His Name!

Breaking through all those layers of cement using our own strength and willpower is about as effective as trying to chop a hole in a sidewalk with a plastic spoon. If we find that our immature opinions, attitudes and habits are "encased in cement," we are not helpless. When we use God's Word and pray in Jesus' name, anything is possible!

PONDERINGS

~ In what areas are you the most stubborn? What are your favorite excuses for avoiding change?

~ George Bernard Shaw (1856-1950) said: *"Progress is impossible without change, and those who cannot change their minds cannot change anything."* What did he mean?

~ How should "praying in Jesus' name" sensitize us to His priorities?

> Lord, my stubborn will at last hath yielded; I would be Thine, and Thine alone; and this the prayer my lips are bringing; Lord, let in me Thy will be done. Sweet will of God, still fold me closer, till I am wholly lost in Thee.
> ~ Lyrics by Lelia N. Norris (1862-1929)

Grandson, Ben Edwards

PURE POPPYCOCK

Our grandson, Ben, in his junior year of high school, along with his classmates, had to write a poem to be published in a book called, "Hubris, A Student Literary Journal." The word hubris means, "The excessive pride and ambition that usually leads to the downfall of a hero in classical tragedy." Ben's poem, "Understanding," was voted by his classmates as one of the best in the class saying it was an excellent and profound piece of poetry. Here is his poem:

UNDERSTANDING
by Ben Edwards

Mom understands when elephant takes something.
She cries through what was once the window.
The white water jumps with the whisper of the sad story.
Of magic and butterflies, Of pumpkins and stars.
Dad understands when dishwasher runs away.
He yells through what once was the light.
The white rapids roll with the singing of the mad glory.
Of war and sleeping, Of defeat and noise.

What they didn't know is that Ben used an online kid's scrabble type of website that allows the user to move letters around to make random words and sentences. There is NO deep profound meaning behind the poem. It's simply a bunch of nonsensical random statements - nothing more than pure poppycock!

I wonder how often we ascribe value to things on this earth that are nonsensical to God. We admire those with outward beauty even when they do not display a beautiful spirit on the inside. We look up to those who have accumulated great riches whether or not they have accumulated God's wisdom. We value those in high position while God values those who are willing to be servants.

The Apostle Paul, in Romans 1:21-23 (MSG), talks about the "pure poppycock" of those who value the world more than God:

"People knew God perfectly well, but when they didn't treat him like God, refusing to worship him, they trivialized themselves into silliness and confusion so that there was neither sense nor direction left in their lives. They pretended to know it all, but were illiterate regarding life. They traded the glory of God who holds the whole world in his hands for cheap figurines you can buy at any roadside stand." May God give us the wisdom to see the world through His eyes.

PONDERINGS

~ Read Matthew 6:31-34. What does this tell us about God's priorities?

~ Read Matthew 10:29-31. How does seeing yourself through God's eyes give us hope?

~ Read 2 Timothy 3:16. How do I measure how much value I put on God's Word? Read Psalm 19:9-10.

O boundless Wisdom, God most high, Maker of the earth and sky, let faith discern the eternal Light beyond the darkness of the night, and through the mists of falsehood see the path of truth revealed by Thee. Amen.   ~ Lyrics by unknown author, 6th Century

Granddaughters, Meghan and Colleen Malone did Irish Dances
at my mother's (Esther) 100th birthday party

WANNA DANCE?

Do you like to dance? Dancing has been an important part of
history, used for celebrations and entertainment even in the earliest
civilizations. Dancing figures have been found etched on cave
walls even from prehistoric times. Dance was a major method of
passing down stories from one generation to another.

Our granddaughters, Meghan and Colleen, did Irish Step Dancing,
which is a traditional dance of Ireland. Step dancing is performed
mostly on the toes, with the torso and arms kept straight and
vertical. There are many different types: jigs, reels, hornpipes,
treble jigs, set dances and slip jigs.

My mother's 100th birthday party was held at Aldersgate United
Methodist Church in Marion, Illinois in 2009. Meghan and Colleen
delighted the audience by performing several Irish dances. They
were stunning in their fancy dresses full of elaborate embroidery.
They wore perfectly curled wigs that added a bouncy, energetic
look as the curls bobbed up and down with each step. Irish Step
Dancing has spread throughout the world. "Riverdance," a

27

theatrical show consisting of traditional Irish Step Dancing, began on stage years ago in Dublin, Ireland and is still inspiring audiences today.

Dancing is a great way to tone the body and develop strong muscles. We need strong spiritual muscles as well. What kind of dance pleases God? Does He expect us to jump up on the tabletops at a church potluck and do a dance that says, *"Look at me! I'm sooo spiritual!"*? Of course not! Instead, God wants a dance that will glorify Him - a dance that uses the spiritual muscles of obedience and humility.

Just as physical dancing is a great way to develop strong muscles, our obedience to the voice of the Spirit will develop strong spiritual muscles. When our spiritual dance develops to the point of keeping in step with the rhythm of the Spirit, it becomes a dance of grace and beauty that is pleasing to God.

I love Psalm 90:14 from the Message Bible: *"Surprise us with love at daybreak; then we'll skip and dance all the day long."* Does God surprise us with love at daybreak? You bet He does – without fail, every morning! Wanna dance?

PONDERINGS

~ Are you a dancer or do you have two left feet? Which kind of dancing do you enjoy most?

~ What happens to muscles that are not used? Which spiritual muscles in Christians tend to be the weakest and how do we strengthen them?

~ James Dillet Freeman (1912-2003) said: "Prayer is spiritual exercise and every act of prayer stretches the soul." How does that work?

O LORD, be my help. You turned my wailing into dancing; you removed my sackcloth and clothed me with joy, that my heart may sing to you and not be silent. Amen.   ~ Psalm 30:10-12

Grandson, Jake Murphy

SEE THE BIG PICTURE

Our grandson, Jacob, had an opportunity during college to go to Ireland on a mission trip in 2008. He shares the following:

God provided numerous opportunities for me to show the love of God to many people in Ireland. I was privileged to talk with an Irish woman whose cousin was suffering from an addiction to drugs. I was able to encourage her and inform her of a Teen Challenge meeting at one of the local churches. God also blessed me in conversations with many teenagers and He confirmed the call He has placed on my life to work with them.

Being in Ireland opened my eyes to more of the spiritual world than before, and showed me the immense importance prayer plays in our everyday lives. The trip helped me to see more of what God wants me to do and how He wants me to do it. One way I am pursuing His plan is a college minor for Inter-Cultural Studies/Missions. With this, I hope to inspire youth to work in the mission field and help evangelize the youth of the world.

Jake sees the big picture. He sees himself as part of the larger plan of God. He has a vision of the vast possibilities for mission - not just to the youth in his neighborhood, but also to youth everywhere.

In our own lives, we often have tunnel vision. Years ago, I had a fear of flying by myself. It was not the usual fear of an airplane ride, but a fear of getting lost in the airport. I tend to be a bit "directionally impaired" and I feared going down the wrong concourse, ending up in the wrong terminal at the wrong gate and eventually on the wrong plane. My husband taught me how to get the big picture. He told me to stand still and take my time to see all the signs before I went charging off down a concourse.

Instead of charging down the hallway of good intentions, we need to stand still and meditate on all the signs God has given us that lead to His master plan for our lives. Ephesians 1:18-19 says it best from the Message Bible:

> I ask the God of our Master, Jesus Christ, the God of glory, to make you intelligent and discerning in knowing him personally, your eyes focused and clear, so that you can see exactly what it is he is calling you to do, grasp the immensity of this glorious way of life he has for his followers, oh, the utter extravagance of his work in us who trust him - endless energy, boundless strength!

Then we will be able to see the big picture!

PONDERINGS

~ In what ways does our society miss the big picture?

~ What do you think God's master plan is for YOUR life, as you understand it?

~ Read 1 John 2:15-17. How does this scripture encourage us to see the big picture?

O God, Immortal and Invisible, forgive the faltering faith of those whose dwelling is among the mortal and the seen. The heavens may declare Thy glory, but our eyes are too earthbound to read their story of infinity and peace. O Lord, that we might receive our sight. Amen.   ~ W. E. Orchard (1877-1955)

Son, Bruce Edwards with a Broadhead Skink

THE BITES OF LIFE

Have you ever been bitten? When I was a baby, I was bitten by a rat. My mother heard me screaming and rushed into the nursery. When she turned on the light, she saw a large rat jumping out of my crib after it had bitten the palm of my hand!

At the age of five, I was playing in a small creek near our house and saw a large turtle. I decided to take it home to show my mommy. I put my hands on either side of the shell and picked it up only to have the snapping turtle's head shoot out and bite the back of my hand before I knew what was happening. I dropped that turtle and ran home crying hysterically.

When our children were small, our family spent a lot of time camping. Anyone who has gone camping is quite familiar with the "bites of life!" I've had my share of insect bites – chiggers, mosquitoes, black flies, horse flies and ticks. I vividly remember one camping trip in the Upper Peninsula of Michigan. The no-see-ums were driving us crazy. A no-see-um is a biting midge. It is a bloodsucker many times smaller than a mosquito but with a bite much more painful. They are very easy to kill – just smash them with your finger. This works well IF you see one. The problem is they are so small, you "no-see-um" until you feel the bite! They were small enough to go through the screens in our camper. At night, even with the covers up to my chin, I would suddenly jump from the sharp pinprick of a no-see-um biting me on the cheek and would spend the rest of the night with my head under the covers.

The "bites of life" are sometimes dangerous, sometimes physically or emotionally painful and sometimes just plain irritating, but everyone has them. No one is immune. The Apostle Paul had his share of "bites" in his lifetime. He was imprisoned, flogged, exposed to death, beaten, stoned, gone without sleep, gone without food and water and had been cold and naked. Did that stop him from preaching the gospel? Absolutely not! He said in Philippians 3:14: *"I press on toward the goal to win the prize for which God has called me heavenward in Christ Jesus."*

When the "bites of life" come...and they will...we do not have the option to use them as excuses to whine, complain or give up. We, along with the Apostle Paul, can *"press on toward the goal"* and God will be with us every step of the way.

PONDERINGS

~ What irritates you the most? How do these irritations side-track you from your goals? What is the best way to get back on track?

~ Rumi (1207-1273) said: *"If you are irritated by every rub, how will your mirror be polished?"* What did he mean?

~ Read 2 Corinthians 4:8-9. In what ways do these verses describe a "mature" Christian?

O God, we come to You with our noisy lives, our petty irritations, our weaknesses, our sins. Lord, help us, help us at this time as we try in the midst of the wreckage to build something worthy of Your goodness. We ask in the Name of our Lord and Savior, Jesus Christ. Amen   ~ Frank W. Gunsaulus (1856-1921)

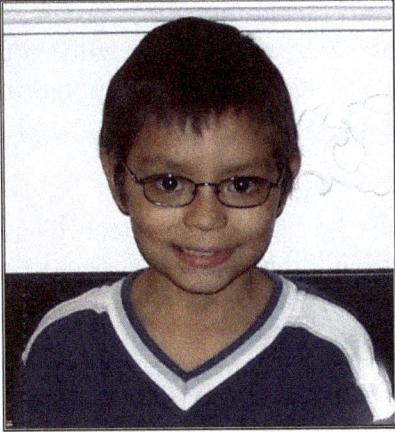

Grandson, David Andersen

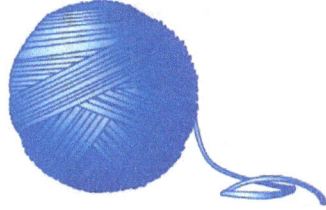

NO STRINGS ATTACHED

When our grandson, David, was eight years old, he loved playing computer games. Before I let him play on the computer, he first had to have a piano lesson. I quickly found David's enthusiasm for piano lessons didn't quite match mine. When I would tell him it was time for his lesson, he sometimes responded, *"But I don't want to!"* David quickly became familiar with my reply, *"OK David, you don't have to if you don't want to, but there's a string attached from the piano to the computer."* He soon learned what that meant... if he didn't practice piano, he would not have the privilege of playing games on the computer. So now if I say, *"That's okay, David, you don't have to if you don't want to,"* he responds with, *"I know, I know. There's a string attached. I want to."* Although his computer time was limited to one hour, those strings came in mighty handy.

There are many things in life that have strings attached. Sometimes we look at our responsibilities and say, *"I don't want to."* But if we do not accomplish what the boss wants, we may lose our job. If we don't brush our teeth, we may get cavities. If we don't obey the law, we may find ourselves in jail. If we don't do the homework, we may fail the test. There are strings attached.

Other areas should also have a "NO strings attached" policy. One of those is in our giving. We don't give to get. God calls us to be generous givers, not for the sake of getting something in return, but simply to share with others in need because God has shared with us.

Another place where there should be "no strings attached" is the area of love. We do not tell our children, *"If you do what I want you to do, I will love you."* Or... *"If you get A's on your report card, I will love you."* We may sometimes be unhappy with our children's behavior, but we love them unconditionally no matter what they do.

The same is true of God. We are God's children and we do many things that displease our Heavenly Father. But He loves us unconditionally. Romans 5:8 tells us that. *"God demonstrates his own love for us in this: While we were still sinners, Christ died for us."* The Message Bible says it this way: *"God put his love on the line for us by offering his Son in sacrificial death while we were of no use whatever to him."* There are "no strings attached."

PONDERINGS

~ Was there a time someone gave you a generous gift with no strings attached? Why do you think they did it?

~ God says, *"Hey, I will take all your mistakes, all your guilt and give you a fresh start. No strings attached."* How does that make you feel? What should be our response?

~ Read 1 Peter 1:22. How does a sincere, deep love eliminate the need to attach strings? In what areas are we most tempted to attach strings to our love for others?

O to grace how great a debtor, daily I'm constrained to be! Let Thy goodness, like a fetter, bind my wandering heart to Thee. Prone to wander, Lord, I feel it; prone to leave the God I love; here's my heart, O take and seal it, seal it for Thy courts above. Amen.
~ Lyrics by Robert Robinson (1735-1790)

Fruit Pizza made by daughter, Rhonda Andersen

WHAT'S IN YOUR MOUTH?

God designed our mouths with taste buds to give us satisfaction and appreciation for good food. They also tell us when the food is not so good. Our son, Bruce shares this story:

My wife, Mary, owned and operated a licensed day care in our home for many years. With tough budgets, she liked to save money by making her own play dough. We had some yellow popcorn oil in the pantry that she thought might work well for her play dough recipe. When the play dough was done, the popcorn oil had colored the play dough so it looked just like cookie dough. The wheels began to turn in Mary's head. She knew I liked raw cookie dough, so she and Sharon, her employee, hatched a plan.

Mary hustled out to the store to buy some chocolate chips. Back home, Mary mixed the chocolate chips into the play dough, moistened the edge of the bowl and sprinkled it with flour, placed a piece of wax paper over the "cookie dough" and placed the bowl in the fridge. All afternoon, they chuckled to themselves thinking of the poor victim (me) who would soon be home from work.

35

When I finally arrived home, I followed my typical routine, putting my things down and heading straight for the fridge for a snack. When I opened the door and saw the cookie dough, my eyes lit up! Not wanting to eat in front of the day care children who were still around, I grabbed a handful, hid it from sight until I was in the hallway and then threw it into my mouth.

If you are not familiar with powdered alum, an ingredient in Mary's play dough, alum immediately sucks the moisture out of the mouth and acts like the worst puckerer ever. Boy, was I surprised! The worst part was knowing I'd been had and having to listen to Mary's and Sharon's roaring laughter.

We laugh at this comical incident because what Bruce put into his mouth did not belong there. Our mouths are also designed for communication, but some of the words we allow to form there do not belong either. Words of anger, untruth, pride, self-pity or greed have a way of turning bitter just like alum.

The Bible gives us good advice: *"Do not let any unwholesome talk come out of your mouths, but only what is helpful for building others up according to their needs, that it may benefit those who listen."* ~ Ephesians 4:29

PONDERINGS

~ What's in YOUR mouth? What are some examples of "wholesome" talk?

~ Re-read Ephesians 4:29. What do you think would be considered "unwholesome" talk?

~ Read Luke 6:45. If someone listened to everything you said for a day, what conclusions would they come to about the condition of your heart? How do we change from the inside out?

Set a guard over my mouth, O LORD; keep watch over the door of my lips. Let the words of my mouth and the meditation of my heart be acceptable in your sight, O Lord, my rock and my Redeemer. Amen. ~ Psalm 141:3 and Psalm 19:14

APPLES OF GOLD

"A word aptly spoken is like
apples of gold in settings of silver."
Proverbs 25:11

Like apples of gold in settings of silver,
Let my words please you each day;
For I am accountable to you, O Lord
For every word that I say.

Let my speech be seasoned with salt,
Filled with compassion divine;
Carefully choosing the words that I say,
May they be gracious and kind.

Help me redeem each moment of time,
Avoiding idle chatter;
Help me to focus my heart and my mind
On things that really matter.

Give me the courage to speak the truth,
Exalting your Name above;
To shout from the rooftops, "How awesome You are!"
Extolling the depths of your love.

Like apples of gold in settings of silver,
Let my words please you each day;
For I am accountable to you, O Lord
For every word that I say.

~ Idella Pearl Edwards

"Feed your faith and your fears
will starve to death."

~Author Unknown

Grandson, Zac Benson

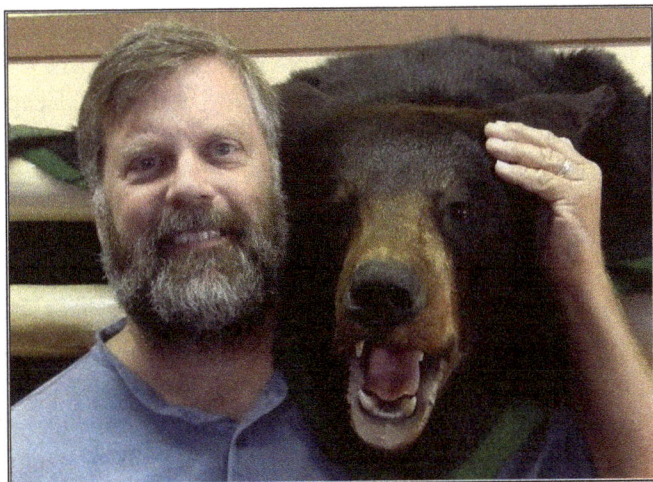
Son, Bruce Edwards (the one on the left)

CONTROL YOUR MONSTERS

Our son, Bruce, never seemed to be afraid of monsters. And, our daughter, Kerry, learned to control her monsters at a very early age. Kerry shares the following:

> When I was six years old, I lived in a place that had a large number of stray dogs who had grown distrustful of people. But somehow, much to my parents dismay, this innocent, naïve child became very good at breaking down the distrust of those dogs and, one by one, each became my friend.

> Fast forward a few years and you'll find a nine-year-old girl now living in a new state, feeling very out of place in her strange new surroundings. As that feeling filtered into my dreams I began having recurring nightmares. In the nightmare wild monsters would surround my home threatening and scaring me. But every single time, every time I dreamt this, I would summon my courage and bravely approach the monsters. Somehow I was able to bridge the gap of misunderstanding and their aggressiveness would disappear. Suddenly my dream was no longer a nightmare but a wonderful frolic with my newfound friends.

Kerry learned how to control her monsters. When our grandchildren, David and Christine, were small, they knew how to control monsters as well. They both loved music and especially enjoyed "The Phantom of the Opera." Their favorite part was the "scary music" and when played, I had to pretend to be the Phantom and chase them all through the house.

They had two methods of escape. 1) If one of them could sneak back to the music player and switch the music to a sweetly sung song called, "Think of Me," the Phantom must instantly become nice. 2) The other method was for them to hide in the hall closet. When I open the closet door, Christine would come out hobbling on a walking cane pretending to be an old woman. Then I was supposed to ask her, *"Madam, have you seen two delicious-looking children?"* She would deny it, throw down the cane, and both would run away. They never tired of this game. (Grandma did, of course.) But they did a great job of controlling their monsters.

How well do you control YOUR monsters? Do the monsters of fear and doubt intimidate you? Kerry controlled her monsters by creating positives out of negatives. With God's help, we can do the same because, *"God gave us a spirit NOT of fear but of power and love and self-control."* (2 Timothy 1:7)

PONDERINGS

~ What were you most afraid of as a child? What do you worry about most as an adult? Family? Finances? Health?

~ How do our fears steal our "hopes and dreams"?

~ Eleanor Roosevelt (1884-1962) said: *"You gain strength, courage and confidence by every experience in which you really stop to look fear in the face. You must do the thing you think you cannot do."* When did you look fear in the face?

Yea, though I walk through the valley of the shadow of death, I will fear no evil: for thou art with me; thy rod and thy staff they comfort me. Amen. ~ Psalm 23:4

"I love that his massive paws were folded just like he was stopping to pray."
St. Louis Zoo photo by Rebecca Odle

BEARY GOOD

My friend, JoAnne Swafford, tells of her experience:

It was a cool morning for mid-July in the Upper Peninsula of Michigan - a nice day for picking raspberries. Reluctantly, all six kids, ages 6 thru 12, would grab berry pails made from 1-lb. coffee cans. When we'd whine about spending our summer picking berries, my mother would remind us that in the dead of winter, while eating berry pie, we'd be glad we spent the summer working instead of playing.

Today we would be picking along the railroad tracks. This is where the largest wild berries grew. Mother had her eye on that patch of berries ever since she saw the blossoms in the spring. Six kids and my mother, with her double-barreled shotgun over her shoulder, set off for a berry-pickin' day. I didn't know who Annie Oakley was but the family would tease her by calling her that. We felt safe knowing that gun was over her shoulder.

Along the tracks was an uphill grade with tall grass and thick bushes. Big red raspberries were hanging from them. Mother lined us up like a drill sergeant, spacing us a few yards from each other. We knew the ritual. We picked as far as we could to the left, then to the right, and of course in front as far as our

41

arms could reach. And we'd better pick our space clean!

Every once in a while, my mother would call our names and ask how we were doing. When she got to my sister - no answer. After a few calls she spread the bushes wide and yelled, *"ANSWER ME!!!"* To her shock, she looked directly into the face of a black bear standing on his hind legs, his mouth full of berries. With a growl, the bear took off down to the railroad tracks and into the woods as fast as he could go, but not before stumbling over the gun that was laying on the tracks that my mother brought with us just in case we came upon a bear.

JoAnne's story is a "beary good" example of the shocking surprises Satan sends our way to derail our good intentions. He hides in the bushes of our apathy and carelessness. We may frighten him away for a while with our own efforts, but he will be back. We need the power of God's Word within reach. We would never leave our Bible laying on the railroad tracks, but we may leave it on a shelf collecting dust. The very best place to keep God's Word is inside of us. Proverbs 2:1 tells us to, "...*store up my commands within you.*" In fact, Deuteronomy 11:18 gives a command: *"Fix these words of mine in your hearts and minds; tie them as symbols on your hands and bind them on your foreheads."* God's Word has power!

PONDERINGS

~ What is the best way to fix God's Word in your heart and mind?

~ Read 2 Timothy 3:16-17. God's Word is valuable for fighting our enemy. What does this verse list as other purposes? How do they apply to your life?

~ Share with the group a scripture that has been helpful to you.

Lord, how sweet are your words to my taste, sweeter than honey to my mouth! I gain understanding from your precepts; therefore I hate every wrong path. Your word is a lamp to my feet, a light for my path. Amen.   ~ Psalm 119:103-105

Michigamme United Methodist Institute Chapel
Photo by Renée Deroche

SURPRISE!

Do you like surprises? In 1984, we were able to pull off a wonderful surprise for our son and daughter-in-law. The previous year, we had attended Bruce and Mary's wedding in the beautiful log chapel at Michigamme United Methodist Institute during Family Camp in the Upper Peninsula of Michigan. Now, they were inviting us to come from our home in Illinois to help celebrate their first wedding anniversary on the first day of camp. We made plans immediately to fly up there, but wanted to keep it a secret so we told them we would be unable to attend.

We sent a recorded message in advance to be played during the event. When we arrived at camp, we hid in a room adjacent to the celebration. Unaware of our presence, they played the cassette tape for everyone to hear. At the end of the message, the recorded dialog between my husband and me went something like this: *"You know, this message is so impersonal." "I agree. What should we do?" "Why don't we just walk through that door?"* And we did. It was a rather emotional reunion!

Surprises are fun. Our loving and generous God loves to surprise us as well. My husband and I coordinated a Lay Witness Mission at Firestone Park United Methodist Church in Akron, Ohio. The visiting team met for prayer in an upstairs room before the evening service. It was a glorious spring morning, the windows were open, and all the birds were singing and chirping loudly. We stood in a circle holding hands. One of our team members, noted for his genuine, heartfelt prayers, began to lift his voice and give God praise. He prayed, *"Lord, at the sound of your voice, even the birds hush their singing!"* At that very moment, every bird abruptly stopped singing and a hush fell on each person standing there! We knew beyond a shadow of doubt we were standing in the very presence of God. It was a holy moment.

God loves to surprise us with joy, with sublime experiences in which we have a glimpse into the eternal. *"You have made known to me the path of life; you fill me with joy in your presence, with eternal pleasures at your right hand."* (Psalm 16:11) He has planned much more for us than just a mediocre existence. If we are looking for true joy, we must take our eyes off the pleasures of this world and turn our eyes upon Jesus. Try it. You will be joyfully surprised!

PONDERINGS

~ Do you like surprises? What's the best surprise you ever had?

~ Read Acts 12:5-16. If the disciples were earnestly praying for Peter, why were they so surprised when their prayer was answered? Does that ever happen to us?

~ What are some things that occupy our time that may cause us to miss God's wonderful surprises?

Lord, grant me the grace of wonder. Surprise me, amaze me, awe me in every crevice of Your universe. Each day enrapture me with Your marvelous things without number. I do not ask to see the reason for it all; I ask only to share the wonder of it all. Amen.
~ Joshua Abraham Heschel (1907-1972)

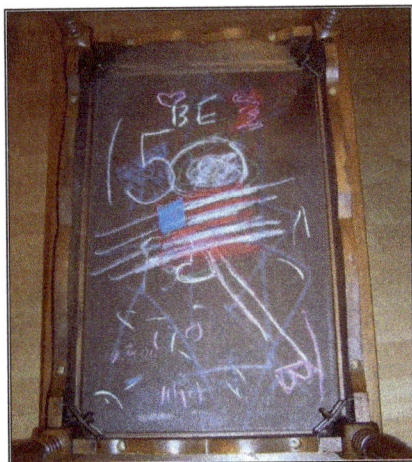
Secret messages inscribed under the end table.

SECRETS OF THE HEART

My husband and I still have some of the original furniture we purchased when we were married in 1960. One of those pieces is an end table. It looks like an ordinary table, but it contains secrets of the heart. If you lie on the floor with your head under the table and look upward, you will discover initials, a child's colorful drawing of an American flag and multiple other symbols and marks. Since I am not in the habit of lying on the floor under tables, it was years before I even realized the markings were there. That means my children had delighted in secretly writing their messages over the years while their parents were clueless to their antics.

We have another table that is one of my favorites. It is not an expensive piece of furniture, yet it is a coffee table that is sturdy and just the right size. It has a storage area underneath where the grandchildren would hide when they were small. (Photos on page 47) The top of the table is filled with nicks and scratches.

My secret is safe because I hide all the nicks and scratches with a decorative coverlet. When I remove the cover for dusting, I can identify many of the scratches, including the ones created by our teenage daughter (who now has a family of her own) when she

45

would come home from working at Burger King and toss her keys onto the table. In other words, one look at that table generates past memories and creates a warm flood of sweet emotions.

Although I probably would have been tempted to be grouchy had I caught any of these memory-making acts in progress, they are now a savored collection of sentimental memories. Time has a way of helping put things into perspective.

The chips and scars of our lives can give us cause for pity parties. They have the potential to destroy our self-confidence and crush our dreams. It is sometimes only with the passage of time that we are able to recognize the way God's hand orchestrated each one with our best interests in mind.

We may tend to be grouchy when things don't go the way we want them to go. We may focus on the moment and miss the big picture of God's grace. But when we remind ourselves how much God loves us, we know we can trust Him to create something meaningful out of every life event. Romans 8:28 can help us see those chips and scars in a new way. *"We know that in all things God works for the good of those who love him, who have been called according to his purpose."* And that's no secret!

PONDERINGS

~ What makes a secret so intriguing? Do you have any secrets known only by you and your family?

~ How do some "secrets of the past" tend to shape our attitudes and actions? Are there some secrets that should be shared only with a close friend?

~ Does God have any secrets? Read Matthew 24:36? What secrets and mysteries did Jesus come to reveal?

O Lord God, Father Almighty, purify the secrets of our hearts, and mercifully wash out all the stains of sin. Amen.
~ Galilean Sacramentary (7th Century)

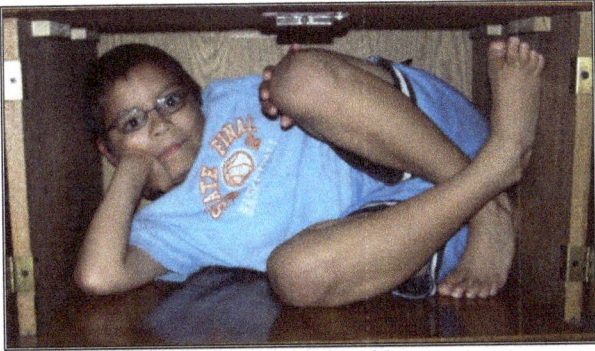
Grandson, David

Granddaughter, Christine

A PERFECT PLACE TO HIDE

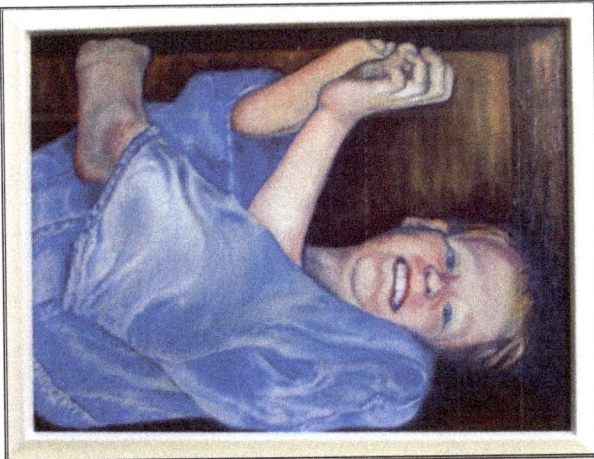
Grandson, Sam (Painting by Kerry Jo Montoya)

Granddaughter-in-law, Courtney Edwards

Love is the master key
which opens the gates
of happiness.

~ Oliver Wendell Holmes
(1841-1935)

Idella Pearl Photos

THE KEY TO IT ALL

One time our daughter, Karen, locked her keys in the car with the engine running. When her husband, Dave, brought the extra set of keys, she began pushing the unlock button on the remote over and over to unlock the door but it wasn't working. (The unlock button will not work if the car is running.) She was totally frustrated and confused as to how to get into the car as she continued pushing the button. Her husband (whom Karen says is the brilliant one in the family) quietly told her, *"Karen, use the key."*

Sometimes, we become frustrated and confused on how to make our life work. We keep pushing the world's useless buttons to make us happy. But Jesus quietly whispers to our soul.... *"Use the key."* What key is He talking about? He said in Matthew 16:19: *"I will give you the keys of the kingdom of heaven..."*

It's really nice when we have the keys in life we need, but it doesn't help if we don't use them. We have all had times when we have been less than brilliant spiritually. God trusts us with the keys to the kingdom of heaven, and we either carelessly misplace them or doubt their worth.

What do keys represent? They represent "access." There are places and things that would be unavailable to us if we did not have the proper key to access them. What does it mean to have access to the kingdom of heaven? The first thing that comes to mind is the option to enter heaven when we die. But when we consider the scripture in Luke 17:21, *"The kingdom of God is within you,"* the meaning goes much deeper.

The Bible tells us God's *"...divine power has given us everything we need for life and godliness through our knowledge of him..."* (2 Peter 1:3) Everything really means everything - every key we will ever need for every situation. When we look into the future, we sometimes see only locked doors and impossible situations. But the "keys of the kingdom" give us freedom "through our knowledge of Him" to unlock our potential and serve Him to the best of our abilities. We will never be a prisoner of this earthly world. As long as we have the *keys of the kingdom* in our possession, we don't have to settle for anything less than His perfect will for our lives.

What key do you hold in your hand right now? What door is God waiting for you to unlock and walk through to a new life of freedom? The "key to it all" is to use the keys God gives us!

PONDERINGS

~ Have you ever been locked out of somewhere you had to be? How did it make you feel?

~ Why do you think God trusts us with the "keys"? Is it possible to misuse them?

~ What door is God waiting for you to unlock? What might be waiting for you on the other side?

O God, stretch me to my utmost - and that utmost means all I can be in and through you; but don't let me cry for the moon. Help me to evaluate what I can be in you, and then let me go out for that goal with all I have and with all you can give to me.
~ E. Stanley Jones (1884–1973)

Sam (rescued from Sam's Club parking lot)
Photo by Rhonda Andersen

CAT GOT YOUR TONGUE?

Our daughter and granddaughter, Rhonda and Christine, decided to bake cookies. Rhonda simplified the process by making the slice-and-bake kind called "tube cookies." Four-year-old Christine called them "tube tookies." Try saying that three times! Sometimes we, as adults, have the same problem with words. We know the words we should say, but we have trouble spitting them out, like we would a tongue twister. The right words are on our tongue but when we try to say them, they come out as gibberish or might not come out at all! In other words...the cat's got our tongue!

Remember all the old tongue-twister favorites? *Suzie sells seashells by the seashore; Peter Piper picked a peck of pickled peppers; A big black bug bit a big black bear, but where is the big black bear that the big black bug bit; Rubber baby buggy bumpers.* Then there are the tongue twisters that may not be as familiar: *A real rare whale; Eleven benevolent elephants; Cinnamon aluminum linoleum; Unique New York; Irish wristwatch.* Tongue twisters really do seem to twist the tongue. Some public speakers use tongue twisters to practice their diction. Working with tongue twisters can build phonic awareness and help develop better articulation.

Tongue twisters are not the only words that seem to get stuck. Many times, the words "Thank you" struggle to emerge in audible form. Some people may feel thankful or may demonstrate their thankfulness with some sort of gesture, but seldom utter the actual words. We've all been guilty of failing to express these words to friends and relatives and especially to God. The simple phrase, "Thank you," becomes a tongue twister to us and rather than expressing our appreciation, we are silent.

Everything we have is from God. James 1:17 says: *"Every good gift and every perfect gift is from above, and comes down from the Father."* The sad truth may be that "Thank you" gets stuck in our throats because we don't really feel grateful. When it comes to expressing our thanks to the Almighty God of the Universe, the problem does not lie in our tongues, but rather in our hearts.

If our hearts are in the right place, the "cat" will be unable to get our tongues. Psalm 22:3 tells us that God inhabits the praises of His people. As we pour out our words of praise to the Almighty God of the Universe, He draws near and fills our hearts with love and peace.

PONDERINGS

~ Would others describe you as a grateful person? How would others rate your level of gratefulness?

~ Read 1 Thessalonians 5:18. How can we manage to be grateful during dark days? Is there any benefit to practicing a grateful heart when things go wrong?

~ Share what you are MOST grateful for? To whom do you need to express that gratitude?

Lord, we thank You for the gladness of the morning, the freedom of the wind, the music of the rain, the joy of the sunshine and the deep calm of the night. We bless You most of all for the ministry of the Son of Man, who by His life set us free, and by His death won us from our sins. Amen.   ~ W.E. Orchard (1877-1955)

Idella Pearl Photo

UNRULY

Our granddaughter, Christine, fell in love with tea parties at the age of four. I found a great tea party set with lots of tiny ceramic dishes at a garage sale. Christine invited Grandpa, Grandma and her brother, along with all her dollies and stuffed animals, to the party. She had an abundance of tea party rules and enjoyed adding more as time went on.

TEA PARTY RULES

1. Hostess must wear her best attire. (Christine's choice was her Snow White dress.)
2. Hostess must serve all the guests first before serving herself.
3. No one may take a bite of food until the hostess has taken the first bite.
4. When sipping tea, one must hold the teacup handle gently with two fingers while holding the little pinkie high in the air.
5. When wiping one's mouth, one must dab gently on each corner of the mouth.
6. No one may talk with food in his or her mouth.
7. Grandpa is not allowed to slurp tea from his saucer.
8. All dollies must refrain from giggling or they must go straight to bed.
9. Each raisin must be nibbled, not gulped.
10. Graham cracker crumbs must land on the tiny plate, not on the table.

We often rebel against too many rules and, indeed, there may be some areas of our lives where rules have multiplied out of control. We would love to be "unruly" in the sense of being free from rules, but it does not take long for a lack of rules to backfire to our disadvantage.

We tend to look at God's rules as a bossy intention to take away our fun. God's love for His children is so deep, so pure, so strong and so uncontaminated from the world's point of view that He made every single rule for our benefit. When He tells us not to love the world nor the things of the world, it's not because He's trying to spoil our fun, but rather because He has something far superior in mind. His purpose is to give us His joy!

"If you obey my commands, you will remain in my love, just as I have obeyed my Father's commands and remain in his love. I have told you this so that my joy may be in you and that your joy may be complete." (John 15:10-11) Jesus is talking about commands and joy in the same breath. His commands are not bothersome nor are they oppressive. God offers freedom and joy through obedience.

If we insist on being "unruly," meaning free of God's rules, we will miss out on many of God's blessings!

PONDERINGS

~ What is the danger of having too many rules? Which rules are important to God?

~ What major blessings might you miss by being disobedient?

~ Read Romans 6:17-18. In what way does disobedience to God make you a slave to sin?

O God, all holy; Spirit of righteousness and truth, we praise You for Your goodness to us. Help us to praise You continually in joyful obedience and cheerful submission to Your will. Amen.
~ A Book of Prayer (1879)

STOP THAT TRAIN!

Have you ever stopped a train? I have! And I did it with one hand. That's the honest truth! This is how it happened…

Years ago, my husband, Jack, my daughter, Kerry and I were on the EL platform on the south side of Chicago waiting to board a train. The train stopped, the doors opened, and we all boarded the train…all, that is, except my husband. He had been crowded from behind, and someone had lifted the wallet out of his back pocket and took off running. My husband, being a man of action, immediately began pursuing the offender.

My daughter and I, of course, were already on the train, and as the train started, I began to panic. First of all, through the train window, I could see my husband pursuing the offender down a flight of stairs, and I was concerned for his safety. Secondly, I had no clue where to get off the train or how to reconnect with my husband. I immediately reached up and pulled the emergency stop cord, which brought the train to a grinding halt. The conductor was not happy! Fortunately, I had acted soon enough before we ran out of platform for de-boarding.

My daughter and I rapidly descended the stairs where we had last seen my husband. We found him on the other side of the gate.

The criminal had escaped, and my husband had no money to buy a ticket to get back in. I was grateful my husband was unhurt but also happy that I had put off my usual tendency to procrastinate and acted quickly enough to stop the train.

Our train is moving! We need to stop thinking we can "enjoy" today and make up for it tomorrow. Today is the day. Let's stop that train! We all know which train I'm talking about. It's the one heading to a place we do not want to go. It's the train of poor habits and poor decisions and poor attitudes, and the only way to stop it is to become a person of action. John F. Kennedy said: *"There are risks and costs to a program of action, but they are far less than the long-range risks and costs of comfortable inaction."*

Since tomorrow never comes, today is the day to "stop that train!" Will you join me? There is an emergency stop cord within our reach. When the train comes grinding to a halt, it will not be because we had the power to stop it, but because the emergency cord is connected to The Source of Power. *"For God did not give us a spirit of timidity, but a spirit of power, of love and of self-discipline."* (2 Timothy 1:7) Let's "stop that train!"

PONDERINGS

~ Are you a procrastinator? What type of things do you usually procrastinate about? How does procrastination cause conflicts with friends or family?

~ Read Proverbs 27:1. Procrastinators are convinced they always have tomorrow. What truth is in this scripture?

~ Does your train seem unstoppable? Where do you find hope? Where do you find more power?

O Resurrected and Living Lord, I would know You and the power of Your resurrection in every thought, every word, every attitude, every moment of the day and night. Then I will live in power and glory. Amen.   ~ E. Stanley Jones (1884–1973)

Asunción, Paraguay
Photo by Missionary John Eisenberg

CHILDLIKE FAITH

Our family believes in prayer. We pray for the pressing needs of our friends, our church and our world. We pray for each other. A few years ago, in addition to praying for immediate family concerns, we chose one family member per week, from the eldest member to the smallest, for special prayer. An email was sent to the entire family, announcing the name of the "Family Member of the Week for Prayer." It also included a scripture dedicated to that person. The selected person then replied with specific prayer requests.

When our granddaughter, Colleen, was chosen, she replied back with a specific request. At age seven, she could have chosen any number of good prayers such as help with schoolwork or the ability to do her best in a gymnastic competition. She chose, instead, to request prayers for her teacher, Miss Nancy, who had lost her son. It was an unselfish act from a very compassionate little girl who believed in the power of prayer.

Children have a simple faith. Why is it that as we grow up, we begin to doubt God's power and His willingness to help. Isn't it interesting that we, as adults, are responsible to train our children in righteousness, and yet Christ tells us that WE should learn from them. In Matthew 18, Jesus *"...called a little child to him, and placed the child among them. And he said: 'Truly I tell you, unless you change and become like little children, you will never enter the kingdom of heaven.'"* (vs. 2-3)

Why would Jesus want us to be like children? Children can be impatient; they require a lot of care; and at times, they can be extremely selfish. On the other hand, they have some wonderful qualities as well. They have not lost their sense of wonder, they accept others regardless of looks or skin color, and they are experts in the "trust" department. Small children will take your hand and allow themselves to be led into the unknown or even allow you to carry them without fear of being dropped. They simply trust. They have the capacity to trust God in the same way and have no doubt that He loves and cares for them.

Wolfgang Amadeus Mozart said: *"It is a great consolation for me to remember that the Lord, to whom I had drawn near in humble and childlike faith, has suffered and died for me, and that He will look on me in love and compassion."* Yes, we need that kind of childlike faith!

PONDERINGS

~ What is the difference between being "childish" and being "childlike"?

~ How would most adults have to change to become like a little child?

~ What does it mean that children have a simple faith? In what ways do adults complicate matters?

O LORD, our Lord, how majestic is your name in all the earth! You have set your glory above the heavens. From the lips of children and infants you have ordained praise. Amen

~ Psalm 8:1-2

58

Grand Teton National Park
Photo by Kim Vanderhelm

HIS MYSTERIOUS WAYS

My husband and I have been receiving Guideposts magazine for over 50 years. When the magazine arrives, the first thing I always read is a section called, "His Mysterious Ways." It tells stories of how God mysteriously and unexpectedly intervened in people's lives in such a unique and wonderful way, it removed all doubt from their minds that God is a loving God and never far away. We also subscribe to Guideposts' new magazine called, "Mysterious Ways." I sent them this story which they printed in their April/May 2013 issue:

I experienced my own "aha" moment from God. My mother, Esther, passed away at the age of 100. I chose two songs for the funeral service I knew she liked – "It Is No Secret" and "God Will Take Care of You." I wasn't sure, however, that I had included her very favorite song. Later, as I was going through some of her things, I found a paper she had written entitled, "His Mysterious Ways," which I have typed below:

My favorite song is "God Will Take Care of You" and I think He proved it through a dream I had one night. I had just traded in my old car for another used car (a better one, I thought) because I was planning a trip. That very same night, I had a dream that I was driving along and had to turn my car sharply to the right. The right front tire blew out and my car and I went over an embankment.

The next morning I was worried about the tires so I took my car down to a place where they check tires and asked them to please see if my tires were good enough for a trip. They told me my right front tire was really bad and the others weren't very good. So I bought four new tires.

On my trip a little while later, I was driving along and a car coming toward me was veering into my lane, coming straight at me. I turned sharply to the right and he just missed me but I had no blow-out...thanks to the dream and my new tires and God taking care of me.

Psalm 121:1-2 tells us where our help comes from, *"I lift up my eyes to the hills - where does my help come from? My help comes from the Lord, the Maker of heaven and earth."* My mother had a personal encounter with HIS mysterious ways. It cemented the truth of God's love in her heart and mind. When we encounter that truth, God's ways are not so mysterious after all.

PONDERINGS

~ Why do you think God's ways sometimes seem mysterious to us? Is there a relationship between mystery and faith?

~ Read Isaiah 55:8-9. When God says that His ways are not our ways, what does He mean?

~ How does God sometimes use His mysterious ways to accomplish His greater purposes? If you could ask God any question about His mysterious ways, what would it be?

Thee, O Great God, we praise! Thee, Mighty Lord, we bless. Thee, and thy marvelous and mysterious ways! Amen.
~ St. Augustine (354-430)

2 + 2 = 4

Do you like math? My husband loves math! He frequently does calculations just for fun. He is sure to inform me the percentage of red lights he encounters while running errands. When he reads a book, he keeps track daily of the percentage of pages he has read. When he was a kid, he enjoyed zeroing in on the square root of a number by trial and error multiplication. This was not assigned homework from school but rather simply for entertainment. In grade school, he was required to memorize the multiplication tables through the 9's, but just for fun, he memorized the tables through the 13's. He is amused when he tells people he graduated in the top 95% of his class and they don't get the joke. Of course, he also graduated in the top 5%.

Once, during an organ recital, I caught him counting the number of tiles on either side of the stage in a college auditorium. He made sure I knew there was an unequal number on each side. In reality, he was at the recital only because I twisted his arm to go, so he attempted to alleviate his boredom by doing math.

I am not particularly fond of math. I can do math, but I look at it as a necessary evil and would never choose to do it for the sake of enjoyment. I definitely never choose to do math in my head if I can locate a calculator.

Math is important to God. Psalm 90:12 exhorts us to number our days. *"Teach us to number our days aright, that we may gain a heart of wisdom."* What does it mean to number our days? If we number the days we have on this earth and compare them to eternity, the brevity of life becomes crystal clear. We have no time to waste.

We procrastinate on so many things. Our theory is to enjoy today because we always have tomorrow. In reality, we only have one lifetime to give something back to God for all He has done for us.

"Teach us to number our days" means we must make the most of each day of our lives. CAUTION: This does not mean trying to cram more into each hour. "Making the most" is all about quality, not quantity! "Making the most" may mean spending more time in prayer soaking up God's wisdom.

Math is an exact science created by God. $2 + 2 = 4$. The equal sign means that each side has the same value. This is also true of the scripture verse in Psalm 90. If we *"number our days,"* it will be EQUAL to *"a heart of wisdom."* Our part is to do the numbering. God's part is to do the math and create in us a heart of wisdom.

PONDERINGS

~ What would you like to accomplish in the next ten years? What would you like to accomplish before you die? Have you been procrastinating on any of those goals?

~ Read Deuteronomy 30:19. How is numbering our days connected with choices and priorities?

~ How would you define wisdom? What is the connection between numbering our days and a heart of wisdom?

Take my life, and let it be consecrated, Lord, to Thee.
Take my moments and my days; let them flow in ceaseless praise.
Take my hands, and let them move at the impulse of Thy love.
Take my feet, and let them be swift and beautiful for Thee.
                           ~ Frances Ridley Havergal (1836 - 1879)

Granddaughter, Destiny Benson

TAKE CHARGE

Our granddaughter, Destiny, is a "take-charge" girl. We live in southern Illinois and she lives in northern Ohio. One night, at the age of six, she told our son, David, *"I'm going to go visit Grandpa and Grandma."* Thinking she was just playing a game, he said, *"OK, go pack your suitcase."* Within a short time, she emerged from her room, bags in hand, insisting that he take her to our house immediately! David had a rough time smoothing that one over.

When Destiny's mom was pregnant with Destiny's little brother, Amanda told us, *"Destiny tells me every time I go to the doctor she wants me to tell him to get the baby out, so I can bring him home. She said she would feed him and take care of him. All I have to do is hold him, so she won't drop him. My precious girl!"*

Taking charge seems so simple when we are young. We just decide what we want to do and try to make it happen. As we grow older, life becomes more complicated. Many times it's even difficult to decide what we really want. Everything appears more complex, and choices seem to have more consequences no matter which direction we go. So we do nothing.

It's time to take charge! Maybe we fail to take action because we know taking charge also means accepting full responsibility. We cannot play the blame game. We cannot make excuses. Perhaps we are lazy and want someone else to do it. Every action needs a leader, and if we care about the outcome, it might as well be us!

Good leaders have these attributes: 1) A good leader is a visionary. Our granddaughter, Destiny, definitely fits into that category. She has no trouble visualizing all the possibilities. If we can visualize the goal, we may also be able to see the steps that need to be taken to reach that goal. 2) A good leader is passionate. Is Destiny passionate? No question there! If the goal is worthwhile, there is no room for apathy. 3) A good leader is faithful until the job is done. They do not give up easily. Did Destiny give up easily when told she could not go to Grandpa and Grandma's house right now? Our son, David, can verify she did not! If we are faithful, we will not stop until we reach the finish line. It's time to take charge and, *"Whatever you do, work at it with all your heart, as working for the Lord, not for men."* (Colossians 3:23)

We can learn a valuable lesson from a six-year-old who loves to "take charge!"

PONDERINGS

~ Do you consider yourself to be a person of action, a dreamer or somewhere in between?

~ Read James 2:14-17. To which areas of life does God call Christians that require a "take charge" attitude?

~ Read 1 John 3:18. What does it mean to put our love into action?

O Immortal King, receive our prayers which at the present time we offer to You from unclean lips, trusting in the multitude of Your mercies. May we not be found fallen and idle, but awake and alert for action. Amen.   ~ St. Basil the Great (330-379)

STOP !

CRASH!! My husband and I were in the living room when we heard the noise. We raced out the front door to see what happened. Our daughter, Karen, had crashed her car into the garage door. As she turned into the driveway, she noticed that our daughter, Kerry, had left a bucket of water in the middle of the driveway after washing our car. So Karen opened her car window and focused her attention on the bucket in an attempt to miss it. She didn't notice how close she was to the garage door until it was too late.

Most of us are prone to believe it would never have happened if WE were at the wheel of the car. Let me point out that we do exactly the same thing. We are going through life on our merry way when, all of a sudden, "CRASH!" Life hits us squarely between the eyes. We didn't see it coming because our attention was in the wrong place. We tend to focus on the trivial to the exclusion of the significant. We focus on the bad instead of the good. We focus on self instead of others. We focus on the imitation instead of the real thing.

In the 13th chapter of Matthew, a story is told of a merchant in search of fine pearls. He found a rare pearl of great value and did not hesitate to do whatever was necessary to buy it. How did he recognize the pearl's value? Evaluation was not made with a passing glance. The merchant had probably spent a lifetime studying the qualities of fine pearls. The more one concentrates on the qualities of the real thing, the easier it is to spot an imitation!

We miss a lot of "pearls" in our lives because we are not focusing on what is true and genuine. Sometimes we are blinded by the intensity of our own desires. Many times, our pathways are camouflaged by the image of past failures or obscured by a fog of self-pity. The pearls are there and we will find them if we focus on *"..whatever is true, whatever is noble, whatever is right, whatever is pure, whatever is lovely, whatever is admirable..."* (Philippians 4:8)

There are a multitude of "buckets" in the road of life to distract us. It's time to bring our spiritual eyes into focus and sort out what is really important so we can apply the brakes in time.

Yes, it's time to STOP! Stop focusing on the wrong things and take the advice the Apostle Paul gave to the church, *"Let's keep focused on that goal, those of us who want everything God has for us..."* (Philippians 3:15 - MSG)

PONDERINGS

~ Which buckets tend to grab your attention? The bucket of greed? The bucket of laziness? Envy? Anger? Pride? Etc.?

~ Henry Ford said, *"Obstacles are those frightful things you see when you take your eyes off your goal."* What did he mean?

~ Read Philippians 3:14. How does focusing on a prize help us to avoid the crashes of life?

O God, my Light, I looked for you in the sky. You are there, but I see you are here too, in the very nature of things. Help me to walk with your green light. Forgive me that I have walked against your red lights. I thought I was only hurting you. I was hurting myself, too. ~ E. Stanley Jones (1884–1973)

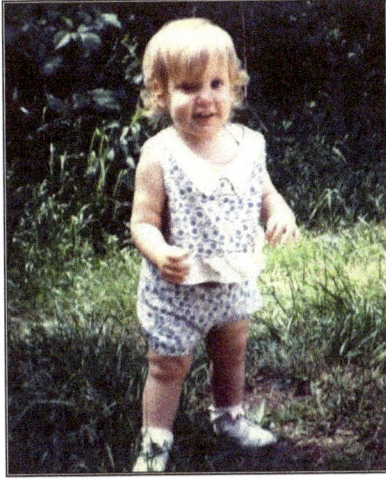
Daughter, Kerry Jo Montoya

MINE!

The Women's Society at our church in Columbus, Ohio asked me to read a poem about daughters at a Mother-Daughter Banquet. I held our daughter Kerry, who was not quite two years old, in my arms during the reading. Kerry had two phrases that had recently become her trademarks. One was *"What's that?"* The other was *"Mine!"*

As I read the poem, she consistently interrupted me. She kept pointing to the microphone, saying, *"What's that?"* I ignored her for a while, but soon decided it might be best to answer her and then continue reading. (The audience was thoroughly enjoying my dilemma.) The next time she asked, *"What's that?"* I stopped reading and said, *"Microphone."* She responded emphatically with a loud, firm, *"NO! MINE-crophone!"* The audience erupted in applause, apparently enjoying her antics much more than the poem I was reading.

Through the eyes of a developing two-year-old, ownership becomes an important commodity to the exclusion of all others. Young children have not yet learned to think of the needs of others or how to share with them. There are adults who have this same warped sense of ownership about many things.

Sometimes that possessiveness pertains to food. Some have been known to hide food from their family so they could secretly eat it later when they were alone. I once read a story where a mother confessed, *"It was years before my children knew that chocolate Easter Bunnies came with ears."*

I have a friend who was well known for her obsession with food. Everyone knew if you wanted to talk with her, it had to be done before the food was served. Once the food arrived, it was impossible to get her attention. My friend's entire focus for the next twenty minutes was on the flavor, the texture and the appealing nature of food to the exclusion of the rest of us. Food, however, is only one small example of our potential for possessiveness.

We all have a tendency, at times, to yell, *"MINE!"* Whether it is regarding our favorite coffee cup or a particular pew at church, we clutch it symbolically to our chest. The Bible explains that everything belongs to God. *"The earth is the Lord's, and everything in it, the world, and all who live in it; for he founded it upon the seas and established it upon the waters."* (Psalm 24:1, 2)

In reality, nothing is "mine." It is all HIS!

PONDERINGS

~ Read Philippians 2:3-4. What do you think causes people to be self-centered?

~ Although everything belongs to God, what things do I tend to consider "mine"?

~ How do you decide how much to share with others and how much to keep for yourself?

O God, our foolish freedom, our feeble pleasures, our fatal self-indulgence suffice to hold us back from You, though You are our very life. Come and deliver us. Amen.

~ W. E. Orchard (1877-1955)

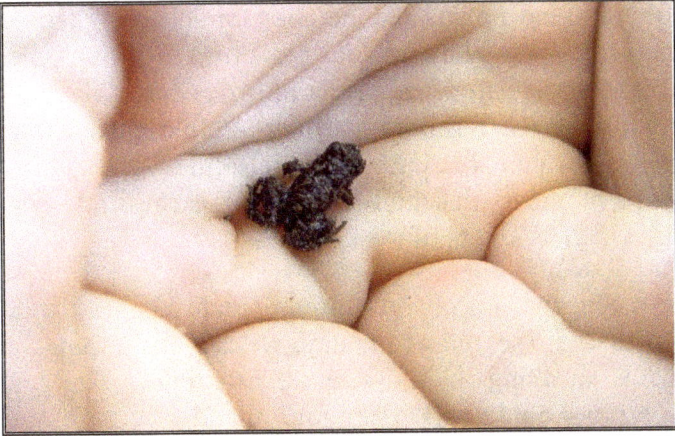

ATTENTION!

Our son, Bruce, told a story about our grandson, Brad.

When Brad was 10 years old and playing for his soccer club, he was one of the bigger kids so his coach was having him do all the throw-ins from the sidelines. It had been raining all week, so the soccer fields were very sloppy with standing water in some places.

Suddenly, sometime early in the second half, we noticed Brad was handing off the throw-in duties to another player. Then we noticed that after Brad would clear the ball by kicking it down to the other end of the field to our offense, he would uncurl his fingers and gently look inside his hand. We finally got his attention from the sidelines and shouted, *"What do you have in your hand?"* To which he mouthed the word, *"frog."* Brad played almost the entire second half of the match with a tiny frog in his hand.

I'm sure Brad's coach would have preferred that Brad's full focus be on winning the game. Brad is now an excellent athlete, but his attention and admiration at that moment in time rested fully on one of God's tiny living creatures. Only God can make a frog, and no one appreciates that quite so much as a ten-year-old boy!

It's important to have plans and methods for achieving those plans, but sometimes, it's okay to deviate from all our rules and regulations to appreciate what's right in front of us. Maybe we can leave the dust on the furniture and help a child catch a butterfly. Some things cannot be put on a schedule. There are those spontaneous moments that pull at our heart strings and beg us to take delight in God's gifts of love.

We have a tendency to charge through each day with a detailed agenda so that, at the end of the day, we can cross things off our list. God is speaking to us. Are we listening? The genius of God's creation should not be taken for granted.

Proverbs 19:21 tell us, *"Many are the plans in a person's heart, but it is the LORD's purpose that prevails."* What's getting your attention? Whatever it is, does it fulfill God's purposes? God may not expect us to stop and pick up a frog today, but He may be telling us to pause and appreciate the small wonders He places directly in our paths.

PONDERINGS

~ Are you the observant type or do you have tunnel vision? How do you decide when it's best to wander off the beaten path and when it's best to stay on track?

~ Is an appreciation for God's created world a learned trait or does it have to be developed? What part of nature leaves you in awe?

~ Does familiarity breed contempt? How can a sense of wonder be rekindled?

Lord, how Your wonders are displayed, where'er I turn mine eye! If I survey the ground I tread, or gaze upon the sky! There's not a plant or flower below but makes Your glories known; and clouds arise and tempests blow, by order from Your throne. Amen.
~ Lyrics by Isaac Watts (1674-1748)

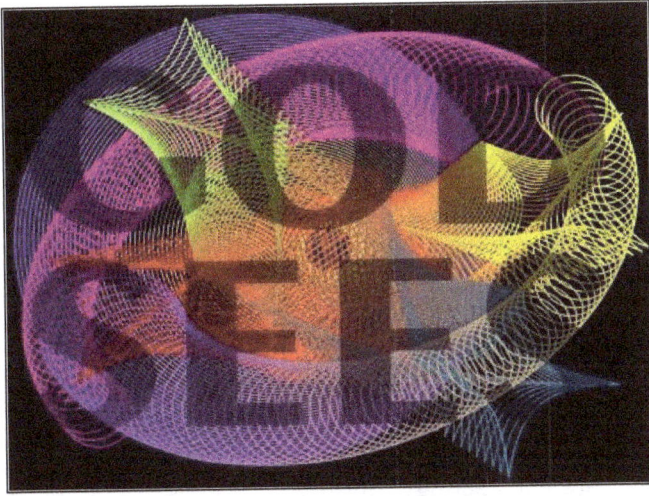

THE GOD WHO SEES

While living in Las Vegas, Nevada, we met some extremely nice people. If I had a choice, however, Las Vegas would not have been my selection for a hometown. It might be a fun city to visit, but we are not gamblers and did not enjoy living there.

One thing we did enjoy was an abundance of out-of-town guests - relatives and friends who had never been to Las Vegas and now had double reason to go there. They could see all the sparkling lights, perhaps even catch a glimpse of a movie star or two, and at the same time, renew friendships with us.

One unique aspect of living in Las Vegas was the frequent sound of police helicopters flying over our house. Many homes, ours included, have a backyard swimming pool with high cement block privacy walls. The walls make great hiding places for those who break the law. The police would frequently shine the bright searchlight of the helicopter into each yard in search of criminals on the run. It seemed to us that the crime rate in Las Vegas was much higher than most places we had lived. Every time our backyard exploded with light, we knew a crime had been committed.

In Genesis, Chapter 16, Hagar fled from Abraham's wife, Sarah, and hid. God found her. Hagar said, *"You are the God who sees me."* (vs. 13) Yes, God is the God who sees each one of us, and He doesn't even need a helicopter with a searchlight.

In the Garden of Eden, even though Adam and Eve tried to hide from God, He saw them and knew what they had done. He sees us as well. There are many times I have tried to hide from God, either by ignoring Him or by burying myself in mundane tasks, thinking He will not notice.

There is a vast difference between the police helicopters with their searchlights and God's warm floodlight that penetrates our souls. The police are protecting innocent citizens by apprehending criminals whereas God is protecting us from ourselves. He knows we can be our own worst enemy.

Job 34:21 tells us, *"His eyes are on the ways of man, and He sees all his steps."* We cannot hide anything from God. His searchlight exposes our self-centeredness and greed. Yet that same light dispenses the darkness of our souls and shines the light of His love deep inside. Yes, God is the God who sees – He sees our heart, He sees our need, and He sees our potential for greatness.

PONDERINGS

~ Is there anything you'd like to keep in a dark corner away from God's light?

~ Why would God need to protect you from yourself?

~ If God floods His light on the pathway to His blessings, why do we sometimes prefer to walk in the dark?

O Lord our God, let the bright beams of your light so shine into my heart, and enlighten my mind in understanding your blessed word, that I may be enabled to perform Your will in all things. Amen.

~ George Washington (1732-1799)

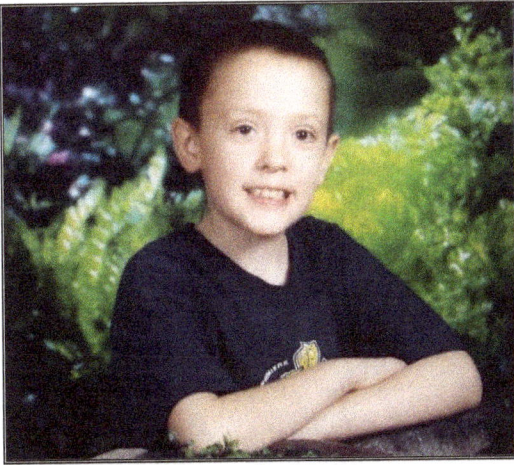

Grandson, Joe Montoya

WE NEED A SUPERHERO!

Our grandson, Joseph, in Oklahoma City, wrote a story when he was in early grade school. This is his story exactly as he wrote it – with the exception of a few spelling corrections.

SUPER JOE SAVES THE DAY

An alligator ate a person that was 40 years old. He was a dad of many children and teenagers. They got eaten by the alligator. Someone has to do something. It's Super Joey! *"You stop it, alligator!"* Then he struck back! He missed and then he did his super blast! Then the alligator dodged the blast but the blast followed the alligator everywhere he goes. Super Joe liked to see the alligator blown to smithereens. And the alligator did! And Super Joe saved the day again. The end.

Why do kids like superheroes? At an age when they are trying to find their place in the world and assert themselves, superheroes allow them to pretend they have a level of power in a world ruled by adults. But even adults like the image of a superhero. Who among us is not disgusted with criminals that prey on the weak, stealing purses from little old ladies and abducting young children? These happenings make us feel helpless and vulnerable. We need a superhero to protect us and fight for us!

There are times when we feel confident and competent to handle the daily frustrations of daily living. But just when we feel we have it all together, life throws us a curveball to prove that we are only human. Our body, mind and spirit are all prone to failure. God did not create us to be infallible. He created us to need Him.

We cannot manage our lives by ourselves. We need Someone who is wiser, stronger and more loving than we are. Isaiah 40:28-29 tells us what kind of Superhero God is: *"Do you not know? Have you not heard? The Lord is the everlasting God, the Creator of the ends of the earth. He will not grow tired or weary, and his understanding no one can fathom. He gives strength to the weary and increases the power of the weak."* We need God!

Billy Graham said: *"It's precisely because the world is so unstable and chaotic that we need God! If the world were perfect, if we never had any problems, then we might be tempted to think we didn't need God. But the world isn't this way, and if we ever needed God's help, it is now."*

Yes, we all need a Superhero. And we have one. His name is God!

PONDERINGS

~ Is it difficult for you to admit there are problems in life you can't handle? Why is that?

~ If God is our Superhero, does that mean we can sit back and do nothing? Why not?

~ How would your life be different if you put our Superhero God in charge? What would change?

Lord, this three-storied house of my body, mind, and soul is yours. Take over charge. Put light and heat in every room, and let the light shine from every window - with no part dark. Amen.
~ E. Stanley Jones (1884–1973)

Grandson, David Andersen

OBEDIENCE FROM THE HEART

When our grandson David was six years old, he was having difficulty complying with his mother's wishes during a particular shopping trip. Rhonda repeatedly told him not to pick up and handle all the merchandise, but in typical "little boy" fashion, David could not resist picking up everything he thought was interesting. After reminding him several times not to touch things, Mommy finally told him to keep his hands in his pockets until he was out of the store and in the car.

David complied for a short time and then managed to "accidentally" knock something off a shelf onto the floor using his elbow. He then squatted down, with his hands still in his pockets, and picked up the object by squeezing his pocket lining material around it. Did he obey Mommy's rules? Yes, in a literal sense, he did. He kept his hands in his pockets the whole time, but he was not obedient to what he knew Mommy really wanted. Although he made some effort to obey the rules, the true desire of David's heart dictated his actions.

Rules and regulations are not usually the controlling factors when pitted against determined self-indulgence. Given enough time, self-indulgence wins every time. We can be ever so determined to

75

follow the rules, but the desires of the heart will eventually surface.

In Bible times, the Pharisees had an abundance of rules. They took great pride in how well they followed their man-made rules and condemned those who didn't live up to their standards. Jesus told them they were paying too much attention to things that really didn't matter. *"Then the Lord said to him, 'Now then, you Pharisees clean the outside of the cup and dish, but inside you are full of greed and wickedness.'"* (Luke 11:39)

God has always been more concerned with the inside than with the outside. In Hebrews 10:16, He says, *"This is the covenant I will make with them after that time, says the Lord. I will put my laws in their hearts, and I will write them on their minds."* We feel good about ourselves when we follow all the rules. It's easier to follow a familiar pattern than to step out in faith and truly obey from the heart.

Just like the Pharisees in Matthew 23:24, we strain out gnats and swallow camels, cross our t's and dot our i's and take great pride in our accomplishments. But when our heart's desire is to please our Heavenly Father, we will not be tempted to wrap our hands around things that are not God's will for our lives.

PONDERINGS

~ In what ways is it easier to follow the letter of the law than to obey God from our hearts?

~ Are there things I tightly wrap my hands around that may not be part of God's will? What comes to mind?

~ In what ways does obedience from the heart give us freedom?

O Lord my God, let me seek you in my desire; let me desire you in my seeking. Let me find you by loving you; let me love you when I find you. ~ St. Anselm of Canterbury (1033-1109)

76

Coal River, Tornado, West Virginia
Photo by Lee Ann Parsons

A RIVER OF OPPORTUNITIES

When we moved to Tornado, West Virginia, we bought a house on the Coal River. The first week we were there, my husband was sent to Green Springs, Ohio on a business project leaving me to adjust to the new house and the new community. There was a heavy downpour for three solid days and the river began to rise. I felt fairly safe because our home was a good 30 feet above the river with a large sea wall. The river was rising at a rate of three feet per hour, so that night I set my alarm clock to ring every hour so I could get up and go outside with a flashlight to check on the level of the river. Fortunately, it only came to within a few steps of our basement door and then began to recede.

The river flooded a couple times a year but never reached our house. Our son, Bruce would stand by the edge of the river and watch all the "valuables" float by that were washed by the swirling waters from the backyards of houses upstream. He tried several methods to retrieve things unsuccessfully, but did not give up. He finally came up with a solution. He tied a long rope on a laundry basket and tossed it into the swiftly moving flood waters to haul in his treasures. Before long, Bruce had a wonderful collection of basketballs and other floatables. He even retrieved a doll for his younger sister.

Although the river was a challenge, Bruce was able to persevere and achieve his goal. We all have our own challenges. It may seem like life is passing us by, and our lofty goals are out of reach. Instead of being persistent in our quest, we accept what we feel is inevitable, and we give up. Harriet Beecher Stowe (1811-1896) once said, *"When you get into a tight place and everything goes against you, till it seems as though you could not hang on a minute longer, never give up then, for that is just the place and time that the tide will turn."*

We, as Christians, have a river of opportunities. According to 2 Peter 1:4-7, two of those opportunities are *"to participate in the divine nature and to escape the corruption in the world."* According to Peter, the only way this can be accomplished is to *"make every effort"* to add the following virtues to our lives: *"...add to your faith goodness; and to goodness, knowledge; and to knowledge, self-control; and to self-control, perseverance; and to perseverance, godliness; and to godliness, mutual affection; and to mutual affection, love."* May we not allow the river of opportunities to pass us by.

PONDERINGS

~ Do you give up easily? In which areas of your life are you determined to "make every effort"?

~ What does it mean to participate in the divine nature? How does this help us to escape the corruption in the world?

~ How can we know whether our diligence is a work of the flesh or of the Spirit?

O God, since You have planted our feet in a world so full of change that we know not what a day may bring forth, grant that we may use with diligence our appointed span of time. Amen.
~ W. E. Orchard (1877-1955)

ON THIN ICE

My husband had a wonderful childhood growing up in the Upper Peninsula of Michigan in the small town of Newberry. As long as his chores were done, he had freedom to go wherever he pleased. He could play baseball in the field with his friends or go for a ride on his horse, Scout. In the winter, he would sometimes go deep into the woods on snowshoes all by himself with a Boy Scout hatchet hanging from his belt and his ice skates slung over his shoulder to go ice-skating on a remote pond.

The pond was about 1-½ miles into the woods and had a spring at one end, which meant one side of the pond was never completely frozen. Being a north woodsman at heart, he knew enough to check the thickness of the ice with his Boy Scout hatchet before he ventured out to skate. He was always very careful to skate only at the far end where the ice was at least six inches thick. He stayed away from the area where the ice became thin and gradually disappeared near the spring. If he had been careless or rebellious, his fun could have ended quickly in great tragedy.

When we wander too far from God's known will for our lives, we are also headed toward "thin ice." It doesn't matter whether our wandering is caused by carelessness or rebellion, the danger is very real. How do we know when we are straying from God's will? Sometimes it's not difficult. When we find our thoughts and attitudes centered on what WE want instead of what God wants, it might give us a clue. When we find ourselves focusing on our own pleasures rather than pleasing God, we can be pretty sure we are wandering away from the solid foundation.

What does the word "wander" mean? It means to roam or stray without a definite purpose or objective. But the real question is why. Why do we wander away from the known safety and security of God's will? I suspect one of the biggest reasons we wander is that we have allowed ourselves to become discontent with all our wonderful blessings and our minds imagine something more exciting and more satisfying somewhere other than where we are. We want the freedom to skate wherever we please in the great pond of life with no one telling us what to do.

The Bible instructs us to *"Make level paths for your feet and take only ways that are firm. Do not swerve to the right or the left; keep your foot from evil."* (Proverbs 4:26) It doesn't make sense to skate on thin ice. If we find ourselves making choices that are not wise, it's time to ask God for His gift of wisdom.

James 1:5 tells us, *"If any of you lacks wisdom, you should ask God, who gives generously to all without finding fault, and it will be given to you."* What a great gift!

PONDERINGS

~ Do you consider yourself wise, foolish or somewhere in between? What is the most foolish thing you have ever done?

~ What excuses do people give for ignoring God's will for their lives?

~ How do I know when I am straying from God's will? What are the clues?

Look upon us, O Lord, and let all the darkness of our souls vanish before the beams of Your brightness. Fill us with holy love, and open to us the treasures of Your wisdom. Amen.

~ Augustine (354 - 430)

DEAD THINGS

In the 1960's, we owned and operated a small motel in Newberry, Michigan in the Upper Peninsula. The office of our motel was actually a sectioned-off part of our living room. The divider between the living room and the office was floor to ceiling bookshelves (open to both sides) with a large fish tank on the living room side, which was also clearly visible in the office. We had several beautiful goldfish, one of which was especially large.

One night some fishermen came to the office to register for a room. They joked that the large goldfish would make excellent bait for their hooks. The next morning, after the fishermen checked out, we noticed the large goldfish was missing. We were outraged. How could they do that! We complained for two or three days, and then one day, we noticed a smell coming from the living room. We followed our noses and found the dead goldfish. It had managed to jump out of the water and land behind the fish tank. We felt so guilty that we had blamed the fishermen for taking it.

Judging by the smell, there was no doubt our goldfish was dead. In the 5th chapter of Mark, Jesus went to a house where everyone was crying and wailing loudly because they thought Jairus' 12-year-old daughter was dead. He told them, *"The child is not dead but asleep."* (vs. 39) They began to laugh at Him, but He took the girl by the hand and told her to get up. Immediately, she stood up and walked around.

What about our dreams? Are they dead? Or are they only sleeping? What is a dream? A dream is an inspiring image of the future that motivates us to climb to the top. Some things are never accomplished without first envisioning their success. Is there a bad habit you would love to conquer? Is God calling you to be a missionary? Is there a skill you hope to develop? What is your dream? God is calling us to dream. He does not want us to settle for the mediocre, but to use our earthly lives to fulfill our God-given purpose. God is able to turn crucifixions into resurrections.

Some of the "dead things" in our lives are not dead, but only sleeping…waiting for us to have faith in the One who specializes in the impossible. Even if they are truly dead, God has the power to resurrect them. In Mark 9:22-23, the father of a young man who was possessed by an evil spirit came to Jesus and said, *"But if you can do anything, take pity on us and help us."*

Jesus' response? *"'If you can?' said Jesus. 'EVERYTHING is possible for him who believes.'"*

PONDERINGS

~ What is your dream? What will happen if you don't reach your dream? What will happen if you do?

~ Harriet Tubman said: *"Always remember, you have within you the strength, the patience, and the passion to reach for the stars to change the world."* Who was she and how did she change her world?

~ What is holding you back from accomplishing your dream?

I know the plans You have for me, Lord, plans to prosper me and not to harm me, plans to give me a hope and a future. Give me faith to believe that all things are possible with You. Amen.
~ based on Jeremiah 29:11 & Mark 9:23

Grandsons, Joe and Sam

FREEDOM

One time, I was at a large mall with my husband, our 15- year-old granddaughter and two grandsons, ages 8 and 10. Jackie and I had to finish some school shopping, so we left Sam and Joe with Grandpa. When we came back, we were troubled to see Grandpa sitting on a bench alone. When we asked him where the boys were, Grandpa (who tends to be slightly on the permissive side) said he let them play on the escalator.

Just then we looked up to see a security guard coming our way, with our two grandsons in tow. It seems they were having fun racing in and out of shoppers and the security guard was afraid they would knock someone down. Sam and Joe abused their "freedom" and ended up not being free at all.

Do you like to be free? Freedom is wonderful. But it is also an awesome responsibility! It is easy to mishandle freedom. I find the more freedom I have, the more likely I will mishandle it. When I have a totally free day, I seem to squander much of the time I could have used for wonderfully creative things. At the end of the day, I'm not even sure where all my time went.

Can you imagine a large city with no traffic lights where everyone is "free" to drive anywhere they pleased? That type of freedom ends in bondage. Seeking freedom from God's rules also ends in bondage. From our human point of view, it seems as though He is trying to take away all our fun. But He alone knows what is best for us, and He loves us so much that every rule He gives us is for our benefit. He also gives us the freedom to choose whether or not we are going to live by those rules.

It might be easier if we did not have so much freedom. Perhaps God should post a daily note on our refrigerator telling us what to do and when to do it. Instead, He allows us to make choices using the brain He gave us. Our brain weighs about four pounds and has 100 billion nerve cells that control our movements, our thoughts and even our emotions. God created our brains with the capacity to make wise and wonderful decisions.

If we choose to ignore God's commands and go our own way, it may temporarily feel like freedom, but we are not really free at all. In John 8:34 Jesus said, *"...I tell you the truth, everyone who sins is a slave to sin."* Slavery is the opposite of freedom. True freedom comes only through submission to the will of God. *"...if the Son sets you free, you will be free indeed."* (John 8:34)

PONDERINGS

~ In what ways do you feel free? In what ways do you feel in bondage?

~ Augustine (354-430) said, *"He that is kind is free, though he is a slave; he that is evil is a slave, though he be a king."* What did he mean?

~ Franklin Roosevelt, 1941, said, *"Every American has four basic freedoms: freedom of speech, freedom of religion, freedom from want and freedom from fear."* How important are these?

You called me, Lord, to be free. Let me stand firm and not allow myself to be burdened again by a yoke of slavery. Help me not to use my freedom to indulge the sinful nature, but to serve others in love. Amen.   ~ based on Galatians 5:1,13

84

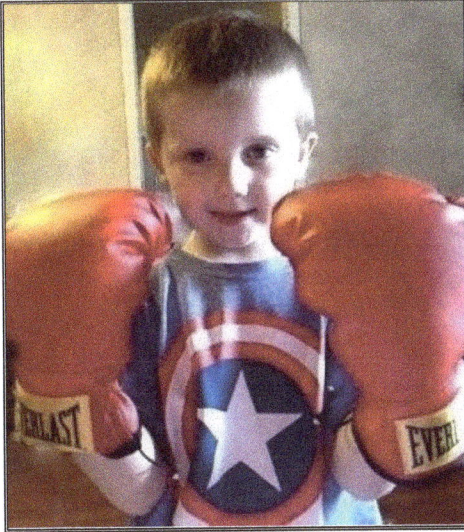

Eli Carpenter
Photo by Sylvia Petrey

FIGHT THE GOOD FIGHT

When I was young, I was never a fighter. I would run home at the mere hint of a squabble. Besides being a big chicken, I considered fighting to be wrong. After we had our first child, Bruce, I tried to teach him not to fight. I also told him, *"And don't EVER hit a girl."* One day, I noticed bruises on our son's back. I discovered that the girl next door (age 6) would chase Bruce (age 5) and pound his back with her fists as he was running away. I immediately talked with her mother and she talked with her daughter, but the poundings continued. As a young protective mother, I did a quick reorganization of my philosophies. I said, *"OK, Bruce, hit her just one time. Then she will stop picking on you."* As it turned out, he hit her once, giving her a bloody nose. The poundings did stop but her mother didn't speak to me for weeks.

We all need to raise our fists from time to time, not at our neighbors, but at the enemy of our souls – Satan. Our enemy makes us feel victimized and powerless. Satan has a knack for making us feel so discouraged that we abandon all hope of change.

The strongholds of our lives can be demolished. We may not win every battle, but with God's help, we will eventually win the war. Then we can say, with the Apostle Paul, *"I have fought the good fight, I have finished the race, I have kept the faith."* (2 Timothy 4:7)

Paul didn't say he fought a mediocre fight. He fought a "good" fight. What makes a fight "good"? Here are five things for consideration: 1) Be prepared! Put on the full armor of God and exercise your spiritual muscles through God's Word. 2) Know your enemy! Be aware that Satan mixes truth and lies together to confuse us. 3) Be in it to win it. Know the serious consequences of losing this battle. 4) Don't go into battle alone. We can't win this battle by ourselves. We need the support of other Christians and the power of the Holy Spirit.

And last but not least: 5) *"In addition to all this, take up the shield of faith, with which you can extinguish all the flaming arrows of the evil one."* (Ephesians 6:16) Are you ready to fight the good fight?

PONDERINGS

~ What kind of physical training do you do? What kind of spiritual training do you do? What would a "spiritual training" schedule look like? Where does "faith" fit in?

~ Read 1 Timothy 6:11, 12. How do we know when to flee and when to fight?

~ Read Ephesians 6:12. Explain this verse in your own words. How is this knowledge useful for winning the battle?

O Lord Jesus Christ, who has called us to put on the armor of God and to take the sword of the Spirit, give us Your grace we pray, that we may fight against all evil and, waiting on You to renew our strength, may mount up with wings as eagles. Amen.

~ Ancient Prayer

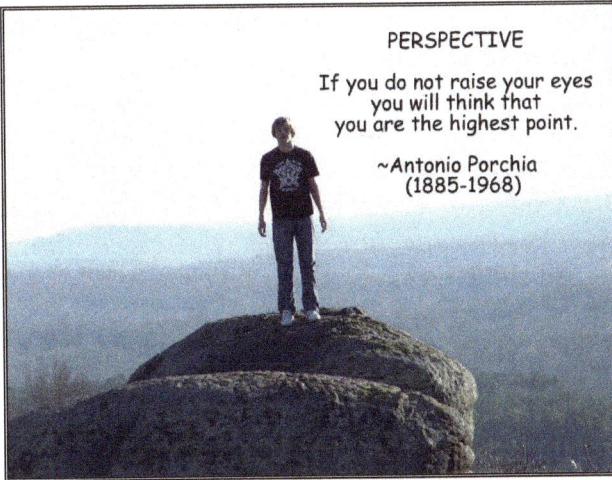

PERSPECTIVE

If you do not raise your eyes
you will think that
you are the highest point.

~Antonio Porchia
(1885-1968)

Grandson, Brad Edwards
Garden of the Gods, Shawnee National Forest

IN PERSPECTIVE

Our granddaughter, Christine, had an operation to repair a hernia at the age of six. Big brother, David, was feeling a little left out with all the attention she was getting. Our son-in-law, Jim, shares the following story…

Last night, as David was probably venting frustration over Christine having received extra attention for her recent hernia surgery, he said he wanted a different sister – a sister he could play with without worrying about keeping a healing incision safe. Quickly Christine sternly defended herself, saying: *"David, there's more to life than just surgery! There's a whole lot of stuff. Surgery is just ONE MINUTE out of everything! There's a lot of stuff in this world, David, and surgery is just ONE MINUTE!"*

(Jim continues) Boy, what a wonderful video it would have made, complete with hand, facial gestures and a whole lot of love! Such a joy it was to see Christine put everything, and I mean EVERYTHING, into perspective by illustrating that even her own operation is only a very small part of life's big picture. What a joyous illustration of wisdom she portrayed!

When our daughter, Kerry, was about the same age, we took her to a drama presentation called "J.B." depicting the biblical story of Job. Since she was unfamiliar with the story, we explained it to her before we went. On the way home, I questioned her, *"Did you understand the moral of the story?"* Her reply was, *"Of course! It means that if God gave Christians all the good stuff, then people would become Christians just to get the good stuff!"* Kerry, although a small child, had everything "in perspective."

We, as adults, pride ourselves on our intelligence, yet we sometimes forget to put things into perspective. Since we have an accumulation of knowledge and experience, it should be easy, but for some reason it's not. We tend to get sidetracked and to make things complicated.

A great way to put things "in perspective" is to put first things first. C. S. Lewis once said, *"You can't get second things by putting them first; you can get second things only by putting first things first."* Proverbs 3:6 (NLT) has some great advice for us: *"In everything you do, put God first, and he will direct you and crown your efforts with success."* Only by seeking first God's kingdom and His righteousness will we truly have things in the right perspective!

PONDERINGS

~ How does it help our perspective to try to see the big picture?

~ Abraham Maslow (1908-1970) said: *"If the only tool you have is a hammer, you tend to see every problem as a nail."* How do our circumstances affect our perspective?

~ How does God's perspective differ from ours?

O my Father, I have taken discipline from too many things. I have obeyed this and that. Result, I have become this and that - and nothing. But now the needle of my life, oscillating in many wrong directions, comes at last to rest in you and your Kingdom. It shall be first and always. Amen.   ~ E. Stanley Jones (1884–1973)

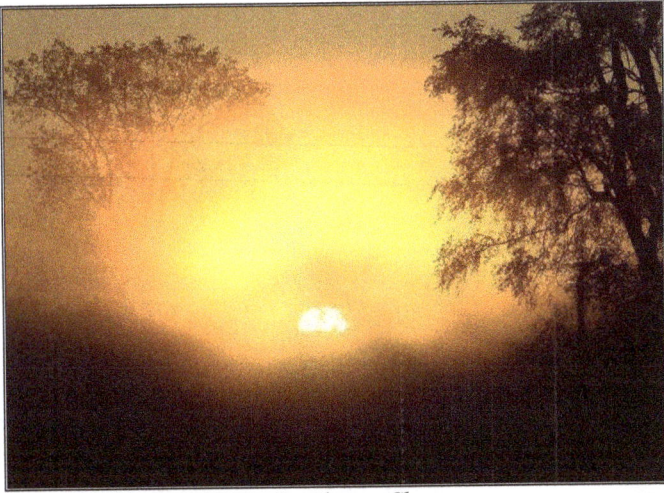

Photo by Sharon Sheron

A POSITIVE LIGHT

Our daughter, Kerry, who worked for Dell in Oklahoma City, took a business trip to Redmond, Washington. On the shuttle one morning, she met a man named Marc who was a CIO (Chief Information Officer) of a large company. When she and her friend, Heidi, went to breakfast the next morning, she saw a couple empty seats at Marc's table and joined him, not realizing it was a whole table full of CIOs. Kerry shares the following:

> Wow! What a day we had! Heidi and I spent the ENTIRE day with these CIOs just soaking up every word they said. It was the most incredible day ever!!! They were so appreciative of us taking the time to actually listen to them and what they had to say. Heidi and I were in complete awe of what we experienced. I never would have expected to end up sitting with men like this, learning from them.

As I thought about Kerry's attitude, it made me wonder how much in awe we are of spending time in the presence of God. Do we "actually listen" to what God is saying to us? Do we "soak up" every word?

89

Kerry went on to say, *"Who wouldn't sit there and GLEAN anything and everything from them?"* I like the use of the word, "glean." To glean is to gather every last bit that is available, not just the big and the obvious. Nothing is wasted. God wants us to glean in His fields of wisdom by spending time in His presence.

The next day, Kerry and Heidi joined a different table to collaborate on some sales scenarios. Kerry said, *"We took everything the CIOs fed us and led the table in designing a scenario and then presented it to the group. Each of those CIOs came over and told us that they were blown away by our presentation because we listened and actually got what they were saying."* I wonder if God would be blown away if we actually "got" what He was saying.

Finally, Kerry told me she was proud that they *"...were able to represent Dell in a positive light."* How often do we represent God in a positive light? Our lives should represent the very character of God in all we do – His love, His goodness, His truthfulness, His faithfulness, His compassion and His wisdom. The Bible tells us to... *"Let your light so shine before men, that they may see your good works, and glorify your Father which is in heaven."* (Matthew 5:16). This is truly a "positive light."

PONDERINGS

~ "Gleaning" takes time. In what ways do I "glean" from God and how much time do I spend doing so?

~ How do I represent God in a positive light? Which shadowy areas could use a little more brightness?

~ Read John 3:21. In what ways are "light" and "truth" synonyms? In what way can truth bring people out of darkness?

Bestow your light upon us, O Lord, so that, being rid of the darkness of our hearts, we may attain unto the true light. Amen.
~ Sarum Breviary, (A.D. 1085)

Pack Rat drawing
by
Idella Edwards

THROWERS AND PACK RATS

My husband is a thrower. I am a pack rat. My mother lived with us for 28 years. She was also a thrower. Other than Christmas decorations, they believed if you haven't used it for six months, it's time to throw it out.

I, on the other hand, am a saver. If there is the remotest chance that I might need in it in the future, I want to keep it. I had a beautiful, full-length down coat that I loved. It had been hanging in my closet for 20 years. Most of those 20 years, it was too small for me but I kept thinking I might lose weight and be able to wear it. I did lose weight. But I am now living in Southern Illinois which means most of the winter days are not cold enough to warrant a full-length down coat. I wanted to keep it on the small chance that I might need it three or four days a year. But common sense finally won, and I donated it to the Salvation Army.

Although I consider myself to have the tendencies of a pack rat, I do not think of myself as a compulsive hoarder. Both throwers and pack rats can learn from each other. (It seems God delights in combining two opposite personalities in marriage.) A pack rat tends to be the cautious, sentimental type, while throwers enjoy simplifying life so they are not encumbered with unnecessary burdens. Rev. Paul Leaming, a preacher friend of ours, said,

91

"Whatever you own quickly owns you. If you own it, you have to dust it, repair it, store it, and in general, keep track of it." That's true. But it's also true that there are times things are thrown away that we really need and wish we had not tossed.

So what should we throw away spiritually? Ephesians 4:31 tells us to: *"Get rid of all bitterness, rage and anger, brawling and slander, along with every form of malice."* That makes perfect sense.

What should we keep? We need to save our faith and our spiritual values in a sturdy keepsake container, ready for easy access. We may sail through many days with enough faith to spare, but there will come a time when we have to dig down to our toenails to find an ounce of faith to get us through. The Bible tells us, *"...do not throw away your confidence, it will be richly rewarded."* (Hebrews 10:35) Whether we are a "thrower" or a "pack rat," each individual decision is a matter of a little common sense and a whole lot of Godly wisdom.

PONDERINGS

~ Are you a thrower or a packrat or somewhere in between? What clutters up your life spiritually?

~ Can you be a spiritual pack rat? How? (The Pharisees kept the 10 commandments, but added hundreds of their own rules.) What excess spiritual baggage do people have?

~ Read Deuteronomy 11:18-21. How do we decide which spiritual values to save, and where do we put them for safekeeping?

Lord, help me to turn my ear to wisdom and apply my heart to understanding. I will look for it as for silver and search for it as for hidden treasure. Then I will understand what is right and just and fair - every good path, for wisdom will enter my heart and knowledge will be pleasant to my soul. Amen.

~ based on Proverbs 2:2,4,9-10

THE RIGHT RESOURCES

During the 1980's, we lived in Downers Grove, Illinois. My husband's job afforded him many opportunities to travel to exciting places like Bangladesh, Egypt, Switzerland, Greece, Ireland, Iraq, Kuwait, Qatar, Tanzania and many others. Jack would be gone three to four weeks at a time, so it was necessary for me to handle the finances at home. He was normally the bill-payer of the family. Before he left on a trip, he would go over the bills with me and when his paycheck came in the mail, I would deposit it and pay the bills.

One time I grabbed a deposit slip not realizing it was for the savings account rather than the checking account. I deposited the money and proceeded to dutifully mail all the checks. You can guess the rest. In reality, only one check bounced, but it just happened to be the check for the church, which was embarrassing.

Putting money in one account and trying to pay it out of another is not the wisest thing to do. We do the same in our spiritual life on occasion. If all our time and energy goes into the secular world and we attempt to draw on our spiritual account during a crisis, we will find it empty. It's important to build up our spiritual bank account by spending time in Bible study and prayer. We have many excuses for not doing so, and the number one excuse is usually a lack of time. But if we suddenly had lots of time, maybe due to an illness or a vacation, to be honest, we don't always share it with God. We more than likely would find ourselves reading an entertaining novel, playing on the computer, watching television or chatting on the phone with a friend.

We can extend our sympathy to young mothers, who never seem to have time to drink a cup of coffee before it gets cold, and with others who work two or three jobs to cover financial needs. We all need to build up our spiritual bank account and if we ask, God will provide the time and the means for doing so.

Bible study and prayer will greatly increase the value of our spiritual bank account. The Bible serves many purposes. *"Every part of Scripture is God-breathed and useful one way or another - showing us truth, exposing our rebellion, correcting our mistakes, training us to live God's way."* (2 Timothy 3:16 - MSG)

Prayer builds up our spiritual account as well. John Wesley said, *"I have so much to do that I spend several hours in prayer before I am able to do it."* The Bible tells us, *"Devote yourselves to prayer, being watchful and thankful."* (Colossians 4:2) Through Bible study and prayer, the "right spiritual resources" are always available.

PONDERINGS

~ If I suddenly had an abundance of time, how would I use it?

~ Charles Spurgeon (1834-1892) said, *"A Bible that's falling apart usually belongs to someone who isn't."* What is the best way to study the Bible?

~ What are the main hindrances to a meaningful prayer life?

Lord, I am no longer my own but yours. Put me to what you will. Let me be full or let me be empty. Let me have all things or let me have nothing. I freely and wholeheartedly yield all things to your disposal. And now glorious and blessed Father, Son and Holy Spirit, you are mine and I am yours. So be it. Amen.

~ John Wesley (1703 - 1791)

Idella Pearl Photos

REJOICE IN GREAT RICHES

As a child, I had a recurring dream. I would climb over a tall chain link fence and on the other side, I would dig a hole. After digging for what seemed like an eternity, I would discover money in the hole….large piles of coins of all denominations. I would bury my hands in the coins, grab as much as I could hold, lift my arms over my head and allow the coins to cascade down over me. In my dream, I never spent any of the money. I only played with it and enjoyed having it. We like having money.

Our daughter, Rhonda, was expecting a pay raise. When she received her paycheck and looked at the amount, she was astounded to find it much larger than she expected. For a moment, she was ecstatic; until common sense told her it had to be a mistake. Whoever entered the raise into the computer transposed the numbers and instead of receiving a 15% raise, Rhonda received a 51% raise. Of course, she returned the excess money.

Money tends to make us happy. There is so much we can do with money. On the Funny Home Videos television show one time, it showed a person receiving a fake winning lottery ticket for $10,000. Before they realized it is only a joke, they ran around the room, screaming and dancing and laughing at their good fortune.

Although most of us are not money crazy, we do rejoice when it's not a struggle to pay the bills. There is nothing wrong with that. But do we rejoice just as much or more in obeying God's commands? The Psalmist in Psalm 119:14 was ecstatic with the privilege of serving God: *"I rejoice in following your statutes as one rejoices in great riches."*

We normally don't think of "rejoicing" when we have to follow rules. We tend to think of them as burdensome. We would rather be our own bosses. But if we consider the fact that our God is so much wiser and stronger than we are, and His love for us is deeper than our wildest imagination, why wouldn't we rejoice that He is directing our paths?

His commands are written to give us MORE joy, not less. Is our greatest delight in God's commands or in our own worldly pleasures? Do our hearts rejoice more in pleasing the Lord or in pleasing ourselves?

Following God's will for our lives will always result in our greater good. Therefore, we can celebrate our good fortune because God is on our side. We may even feel like dancing and laughing. When we submit to His will, it will give us cause to "rejoice" in our spiritual wealth!

PONDERINGS

~ How much do I cherish and relish God's commands? How do I show it?

~ In what ways, as a Christian, am I rich?

~ Read Romans 5:3-5. What does this verse tell us to rejoice in? How do you feel about that? How hard is it to do?

Celestial spirit that rolls the heart's sepulchral stone away, be this our resurrection day, the singing Easter of the soul - O Gentle Master of the Wise, teach us to say: I will arise. Amen.
~ Richard Le Gallienne (1866 - 1947)

96

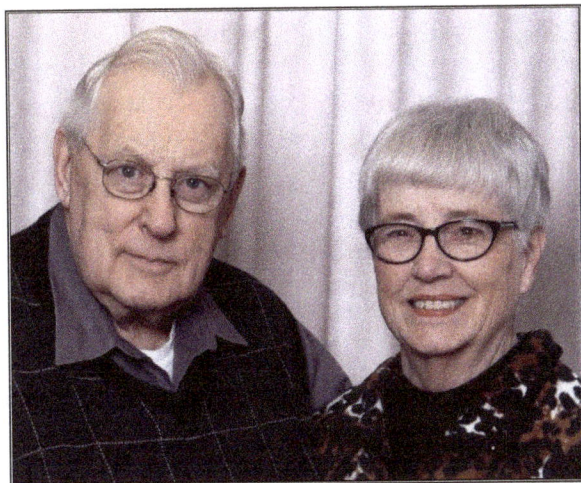
Jack and Idella Edwards
Photo by Stephen Smith

SPOILED

Do you search for ways to spoil those you love with the perfect gifts for birthdays and holidays? I have a husband who spoils me – not only with gifts, but with dedicated service.

Early in our married life, I discovered I had to be extremely careful what I complained about because my husband is a man of action. He is always looking for ways to serve others, and if he thinks I have a need, he will do all he can to help. If it's 10:30 at night and I mention that I forgot to buy something at the store.....before I even realize what is happening.....he has his coat on, heading out the door.

When I am cooking in the kitchen, he will appear every so often and clean up behind me....rinsing dishes, emptying potato peelings out of the sink and setting the table. Of course there are some slight disadvantages to this. If I reach for my stirring spoon, I may find it is already in the dishwasher, or if I reach for the salt shaker, it may already be back in the cupboard. After the meal, he is right beside me helping clean up. Yes, my husband spoils me. Is my husband perfect? No, he has his share of faults along with other husbands, but his good points far exceed the not-so-good.

Are you spoiled? We are not all fortunate enough to have a person in our lives that looks out for all our needs and desires. Some of us have learned to fend for ourselves and have learned it well! But we ALL have a God who spoils us! He is the One who invented the word, "generosity." Why else would He have created all the beauty in the world around us? We love color, but God could have created the world in black and white, and we would be none the wiser. Since we rebelled against Him, He could have left us in our sin, but *"God so loved the world that he gave his only begotten Son, that whoever believes in him should not perish but have everlasting life."* (John 3:16) What a generous and precious gift!

Is my husband helpful and generous because I am a perfect human being? Not by a long shot! Did God choose to be a giving God because we deserved it? Not by a long shot! It was a gift of grace. Does my husband spoil me because he can't help himself? No. He does it by choice. He chose to love me. He chose to marry me. He chose to be committed to me.

God made a choice as well. He chose to create us. He chose to love us. No matter how many times we fail Him, He invites us to return to Him. Our God spoils us!

PONDERINGS

~ If God gave you the perfect gift, what would it be? Or... did He already give it to you?

~ Do you have a tendency to be under-appreciative when someone or... Someone... spoils you?

~ Share a time when you benefited from the generosity of someone else. How did it feel?

Accept, O Lord, our thanks and praise for all that you have done for us. We thank you for the splendor of the whole creation, for the wonder of life and for the mystery of love. We thank you for the blessing of family and friends, and for the loving care which surrounds us on every side. Amen.   (Book of Common Prayer)

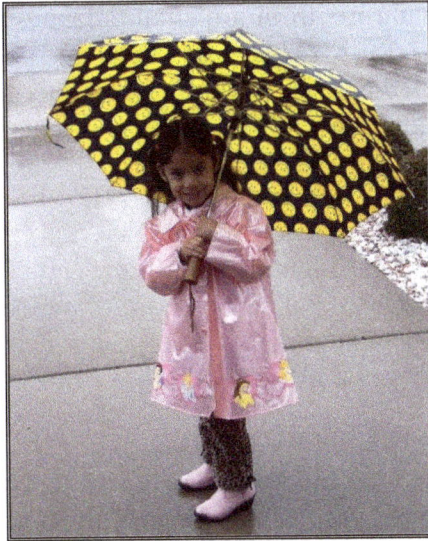

Granddaughter, Christine Andersen

THE COLD DRIZZLES OF LIFE

When our son, Bruce, was a baby, I took him with me on a Christmas shopping trip at Dillard's Department Store in a large shopping center. Evidently, I didn't pay attention to what entrance I had used. When I left the store, I exited on a different side of the building. For obvious reasons, I was confused and could not find my car in the parking lot.

Normally, it would not have been a big deal to experience a little delay in locating my car, but I did not have a stroller and my back was beginning to ache from carrying a healthy ten-month-old baby boy on my hip and heavy packages dangling from my arms as I wandered through the endless aisles of parked cars. Adding insult to injury, the skies began to unleash a cold, heavy drizzle of rain. Little Bruce was vehemently telling the world with a loud wail that he was not comfortable. It was not long before my own warm, salty tears began to mingle with the cold rain on my face as I continued to search for the lost car.

A kindly security guard discovered me in my wanderings through the parking lot. He put us in his vehicle and drove around to locate my car, surely saving me from a mental breakdown. The problem may have been drastically reduced had I planned ahead by bringing the stroller. Or perhaps, if I hadn't been so caught up in the moment and had been more directionally aware of my surroundings, it may have saved the day.

As we go through life, we can't stop the icy rain from falling. We can't always prevent the situations that bring the warm, salty tears. But, by opening our eyes and being aware of our surroundings and especially our own limitations, we may be able to shorten their duration. And we have our own Security Guard who is ready and willing to help us.

When the cold drizzles of life come (and they will!), we can remember that Jesus is our Good Shepherd and will do far more than the kindly security guard to rescue us from our plight. We don't always plan ahead. We don't always pay attention where we are going. But Jesus cares... and forgives... and transforms us... and gives us peace. He offers us abundant life through his death on the cross.

"I am the Good Shepherd. The Good Shepherd lays down his life for the sheep." (John 10:11)

PONDERINGS

~ Read John 10:11-14. What is the main difference between the hired hand and the good shepherd? What does this tell us about Jesus?

~ Can trials promote spiritual growth? How? What do you think the world would be like if no one had any trials?

~ Read Ezekiel 34:1-6. What does this tell us about our responsibility to others?

Good Shepherd, thank you for rescuing me. I praise you for being my Rock, my Fortress, my Deliverer, my Shield, my Stronghold, my Refuge and my Savior. Amen.   ~ based on 2 Samuel 22:2-3

WEAPONS

When my husband, Jack, was in second grade, he received what he considered to be the best Christmas gift ever – his very own axe. It was a beautiful axe with a cream-colored handle, painted blue on the end. Most of all, it was his very own. He couldn't wait to go outside and chop up wood for kindling from the slabs that came from the sawmill.

Another thing he loved during his grade school years were the boots that had a holder on the side for his jackknife. In the early 1940's, a jackknife was considered a status symbol. My husband would proudly walk around with his britches tucked inside the boots and his jackknife within handy reach.

I was also the proud owner of a jackknife in grade school. At outside recess, we girls played a game of splits. We stood facing our opponent and took turns throwing the jackknife into the ground. Holding the knife by the blade end, we threw it hard with a snap of the wrist creating a spin and hopefully making it stick in the ground close to where it was aimed. Wherever it stuck, that's where the opponent had to place her foot. The object was to throw it gradually wider each time so that the other person eventually had to do the splits. The first person to fall over lost the game.

Times have changed a great deal since the 1940's and 1950's. Today, we wouldn't think of gifting small children with weapons or allowing them to take a knife to school. But, in today's evil world, do they need weapons? Do we? We have an enemy to fight. Satan is the enemy of our souls. 1 Peter 5:8 says, *"Your enemy the devil prowls around like a roaring lion looking for someone to devour."*

The Bible, however, tells us that we are to fight a different kind of war and use different kinds of weapons. 2 Corinthians 10:3-4 says, *"For though we live in the world, we do not wage war as the world does. The weapons we fight with are not the weapons of the world. On the contrary, they have divine power to demolish strongholds."*

So what weapons do we need? We definitely need the full armor of God listed in Ephesians 6, but one weapon we sometimes neglect is the weapon of praise. Praise puts our faith into action and will destroy the enemy. 2 Chronicles 20:22 tells us that, *"As they began to sing and praise, the Lord set ambushes against the men of Ammon and Moab and Mount Seir who were invading Judah, and they were defeated."* Praise is one of the most effective, and yet the most underutilized, weapon of all.

PONDERINGS

~ Read Psalm 150. What does it mean to praise God for His surpassing greatness?

~ Can praising God help us overcome adversity? How does it affect our perspective and attitude? What are different ways we can praise God?

~ Charles H. Spurgeon (1834-1892) said, *"Praise is the beauty of a Christian. What wings are to a bird, what fruit is to the tree, what the rose is to the thorn, that is praise to a child of God."* What did he mean?

My heart rejoices in the LORD! The LORD has made me strong. Now I have an answer for my enemies; I rejoice because You rescued me. No one is holy like the LORD! There is no one besides You; there is no Rock like our God. Amen.   ~ 1 Samuel 2:1-2

THANK GOODNESS

On the way to church one Sunday, we were stopped at a red light with a police car beside us on the left in a left turn lane. On our right, a car suddenly whizzed through the red light. My husband said: *"He'd better watch out. That policeman will get him."* No sooner were the words out of his mouth than the siren went on, the policeman cut in front of us and raced after the offender, catching him about a block away. How many times have we seen someone break the law and proclaimed, *"Where is a policeman when you need him?"* It felt good to see justice done.

Our teenage son, Bruce, was working late one night. As he was coming home at 1 A.M., he stopped at a red light on a deserted country road and thought: *"There is not another car within miles and I'm tired. I'm not going to sit here and wait. I'll just go through the light."* After proceeding through the intersection, he discovered that there WAS someone within miles. You guessed it - a policeman! Bruce did not enjoy paying the ticket. To this day, he has no clue where the policeman was hiding.

I got a ticket once too. In Indianapolis, I was driving my co-workers to a restaurant for lunch. I had forgotten my driving glasses and, as I made a left turn, I thought I saw a sign out of the corner of my eye. I asked one of the girls if that was a "No Left Turn" sign. She looked back and replied, *"No, it couldn't be. That policeman is turning, too."*

Some of us have had similar experiences. We could probably write a book and entitle it, "OOPS!" In our spiritual journey, we disobey God's laws for many reasons - carelessness, ignorance, disrespect, rebellion or even apathy. It's easier to figure out why we disobey than to analyze what gives us the desire to obey. Romans 2:4, however, gives us a clue. It says, *"Do you show contempt for the riches of his kindness, tolerance and patience, not realizing that God's kindness leads you toward repentance?"*

God's rules, regulations and punishments do not always inspire us to obey. His love, compassion, tolerance, patience, mercy and kindness toward all He has created stirs our hearts to want to please Him. God is good! Psalms 145:9 tells us: *"The Lord is good to all; he has compassion on all he has made."*

Thank goodness for God's goodness!

PONDERINGS

~ Did you ever get a traffic ticket? Were you sorry you disobeyed the law or sorry you were caught?

~ In what ways do Christians rationalize their disobedience to God?

~ The song, "Trust and Obey" (written by John Sammis in 1887) says, *"...there's no other way to be happy in Jesus, but to trust and obey."* How does obedience bring happiness?

By Your blessed word obeying, Lord, we prove our love sincere;
For we hear You gently saying, "Love will do as well as hear."
In Your wisdom, Lord, confiding, we will follow in Your way;
With Your love in us abiding, 'tis delightful to obey.
~ Lyrics by Daniel Warner (1842-1895)

Photo by Kim Vanderhelm

GOING THROUGH THE MOTIONS

When my husband and I lived in the Upper Peninsula of Michigan, we found the winter weather very "refreshing." His hometown of Newberry can reach temperatures of 30 below zero, and the snow lasts from early winter to late spring. In spite of the frosty weather, as idealistic parents of two small children, we felt it was our duty to teach them to appreciate God's great outdoors, so we decided to take them on a winter picnic.

Our first task was to bundle up the kids and ourselves with so many winter clothes that movement was next to impossible. My husband and I donned snowshoes and pulled the kids across the field on a toboggan into the woods. We rolled the kids off the toboggan and attempted to stand them upright. After wrapping thick scarves around our noses and mouths as a shield from the biting wind, we built a fire and dangled ham steaks on the end of a stick over the flame, all the while trying to convince ourselves and the kids how much fun we were having.

We eventually gave up, ate cold ham and headed for home as quickly as possible. By the time we arrived, icicles were dangling from our noses and we could feel nothing but numbness inside our boots and mittens.

We tried to convince ourselves we were having fun. The truth was that we were only "going through the motions" of having fun. If we REALLY wanted to enjoy ourselves, we should have played Candy Land in front of the fireplace!

When we are chilled to the bone, it doesn't seem possible we will ever be warm again. Bodily chills are not pleasant, but even more unpleasant are the spiritual chills we may experience when we find ourselves going through the motions of religion instead of experiencing a real relationship with Jesus Christ. When we serve God out of duty rather than from a joyous response to our loving Creator, our spiritual life begins to cool, and we find ourselves chilled to the spiritual bone.

"Going through the motions" of our spiritual life will never give us the warm, vibrant relationship with the Almighty God of the Universe that we need. The prayer in Psalm 51:16 (MSG) says, *"Going through the motions doesn't please You..."*

What pleases God is obeying the greatest commandment, *"...You shall love the Lord your God with all your heart and with all your soul and with all your mind."* (Matthew 22:37)

PONDERINGS

~ What adjectives would you use to describe your relationship with God?

~ In which part of my spiritual journey am I tempted to "go through the motions"?

~ Read Matthew 6:33. Why does God want us to put Him first? How easy is that to do in today's world?

Deepen and quicken in us, O God, a sense of Your Presence, and make us to know and feel that You are more ready to teach and to give than we to ask or to learn; through Jesus Christ our Lord. Amen.   (Book of Common Prayer)

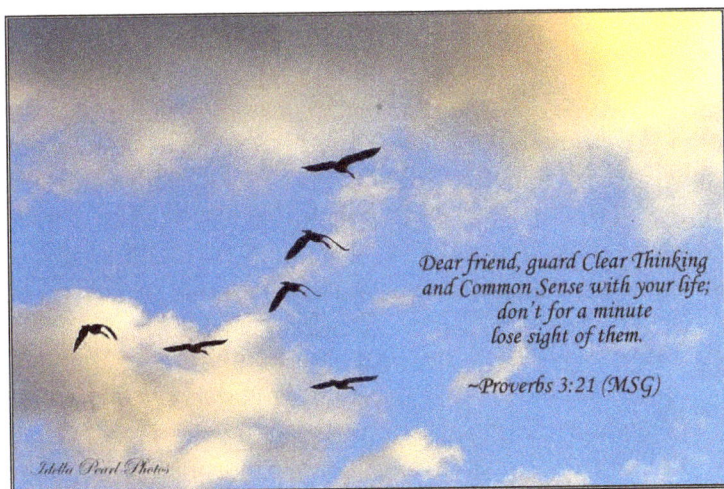

Dear friend, guard Clear Thinking
and Common Sense with your life;
don't for a minute
lose sight of them.

~Proverbs 3:21 (MSG)

Idella Pearl Photos

COMMON SENSE

It was the Christmas holidays, 1958. I was attending Olivet Nazarene University in Bourbonnais, Illinois and I was the only one in my dorm not scheduled to go home for Christmas. I braced myself for the experience of ten lonely, boring days. That day I was thrilled to receive money in the mail from my mother for bus fare to her new home in Newberry in the Upper Peninsula of Michigan. When I arrived up north, not thinking about the temperature difference and wanting to look stylish, I stepped off the bus into a deep snow bank wearing high heels!

It was Christmas morning, 1966. We had written a letter to Santa requesting that he come early because Christmas Day seemed our best option for leaving our home to begin our new life in Columbus, Ohio. Santa was pleased to oblige, and our children enjoyed getting their presents early. We left Christmas morning, pulling a large U-Haul trailer with all our belongings. Later that day we stopped for lunch. As we walked into the restaurant at a Holiday Inn, every eye seemed to be upon us. We were confused by all the attention but it soon dawned on us that, although this was just an ordinary travel day for us, it was actually Christmas Day. Everyone in the restaurant was dressed in their finest attire and we, in stark contrast, were dressed in jeans and sweatshirts.

It was Christmas Day, 1970. Our 8-year-old daughter, Rhonda, was delighted to find an Easy Bake Oven under the tree! She couldn't wait to use it. Our 11-year-old son, Bruce, was equally delighted to receive a set of heavy dumbbells! Anxious to show off his muscles, he immediately lifted them high over his head, falling over backyards on top of Rhonda's pink Easy Bake Oven, breaking off the handle. It still worked well enough to make scrumptious little cakes and muffins, but it just wasn't the same.

Common sense says that stepping off a bus into a snow bank wearing high heels is not wise. Common sense says that sweatshirts and prime rib do not belong together on Christmas Day. Common sense says strength should be built up gradually before attempting to lift the maximum amount of weights in a weight set. Common sense is sometimes not all that common.

Another word for common sense in the Bible is Wisdom. Proverbs 4:6-7 tells us, *"Do not forsake wisdom, and she will protect you; love her, and she will watch over you. Wisdom is supreme; therefore get wisdom. Though it cost all you have, get understanding."* May your life be filled with the blessings and rewards of common sense and wisdom!

PONDERINGS

~ Share a time when you threw caution to the wind and wisdom out the window.

~ How common is common sense? Who has the most common sense in your family? Whom do you admire for their wisdom?

~ Re-read Proverbs 4:6-7. In what ways does wisdom protect you and watch over you? Share examples.

Grant me, O Lord my God, a mind to know you, a heart to seek you, wisdom to find you, conduct pleasing to you, faithful perseverance in waiting for you and a hope of finally embracing you. Amen. ~ St. Thomas Aquinas (1225 - 1274)

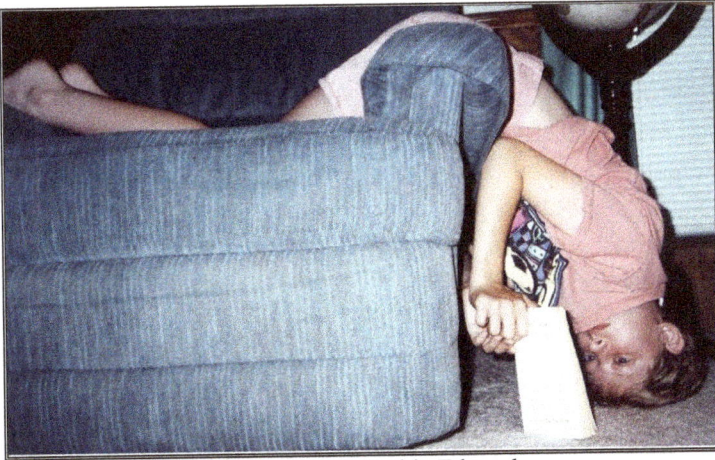
Granddaughter, Jackie Edwards

TALENTS AND ABILITIES

Our granddaughter, Jackie, has loved to read since she was a little tyke. She can read in any position and any location. No matter the time of day, if she had a choice, she would have her nose in a book. I used to be concerned when I would hand her something to read, because she would skim it quickly and put it down. I handed her one of the poems I had written one time and it seemed to me that she barely glanced at it. I grinned at her and said, *"Jackie, whether you like my poetry or not, you should at least pretend to read it to please me."* She said, *"Grandma, I did read it. It's good."*

I'm a very slow reader and it was hard for me to believe that she could read that fast. When an opportunity presented itself for me to attend an Evelyn Wood Reading Dynamics Seminar, I took it. The average person reads anywhere from 200 to 400 words per minute. The course advertises that it is possible to double that speed. They say people can learn to read as fast as they can think. (Maybe that's my problem. I don't think fast enough.) I spent two days working hard in the class and although my reading speed was not doubled, I was pleased as punch with my progress.

When I got home, I decided to show off a little bit to my

granddaughter. Although she had not taken the course, I gave her the timed reading test complete with comprehension questions at the end. She managed to effortlessly make my score look like that of a kindergarten student. Then it dawned on me that all those times she had picked up a paper full of words and put it back down, she was actually absorbing all the material.

We all have different talents. In some areas, some of us have to work much harder than others to get the same results. But God has blessed each of us with talents and abilities. *"In his grace, God has given us different gifts for doing certain things well...."* (Romans 12:6 - NLT) First Peter 4:10 tells us exactly what we should do with them. *"Each of you should use whatever gift you have received to serve others, as faithful stewards of God's grace in its various forms."*

It does not matter whether our talent is singing a solo at church or organizing the church kitchen. When we use the talent God has given us to serve others and bring Him glory, He is pleased. Each of us should be content with whatever God has chosen to give us and celebrate our uniqueness. *"Your talent is God's gift to you. What you do with it is your gift back to God."* ~ Leo Buscaglia (1924-1998)

PONDERINGS

~ What do you consider to be your special abilities?

~ Albert Schweitzer (1875-1965) said, *"The only ones among you who will be truly happy are those who will have sought and found how to serve."* How does service bring happiness?

~ Why did God give different talents to different people?

Lord, our gifts, our talents, all our possibilities belong to us only because they come direct from you. Help us not to belittle these gifts of yours, not to bury them, but rather use them to make you better known to the people of our neighborhood. Amen.
~ Colin Semper, retired Anglican priest.

Green Snake - Photo by Kala Allen

HARMLESS?

I remember the time our son, David, age 12, brought home some baby snakes in a pail. He proudly showed them to us. My husband quickly informed him that they were copperheads and baby venomous snakes are quite capable of causing death.

Another time our children were swimming in the middle of the river behind our house. Although the river was not deep, our youngest daughter, Kerry, was not yet a good swimmer and too short to stand upright in the river comfortably. One of the older children carried her to the middle of the river to a large sand bar where she could enjoy the water safely. I was watching from my kitchen window when suddenly they all began screaming and exiting the river – all, that is, except Kerry, who was left wailing hysterically in the middle of the river. Evidently they saw a water snake swimming nearby. I rushed outside and coerced one of the children to rescue their sister immediately, snake or no snake!

Satan is depicted as a snake in Genesis. Snakes are deceptive. They camouflage themselves and blend in with their environment. Satan is deceptive as well. The Bible tells us he often masquerades as an angel of light. Snakes are also persistent and patient. They will lie quietly for hours waiting for their prey. We cannot yell "Boo" and expect a snake to leave town. They may slither away but they'll be back. Satan is the same way. He may leave, but he will be back. When Satan tempted Jesus in the wilderness, Jesus quoted scripture to defeat him. But the Bible tells us that *"When the devil had finished all this tempting, he left him until an opportune time."* (Luke 4:13) In other words, he wasn't giving up.

Snakes can be vicious. There is a poisonous viper in Africa called the Gaboon. These snakes have two-inch long fangs and can grow to well over six feet. Its bite can kill a full grown human within 15 minutes. Satan can also be vicious. If we look at the casualties in our world, we know that Satan does not possess a gentle side.

But the good news is...Jesus said, *"I have given you authority to trample on snakes and scorpions and to overcome all the power of the enemy; nothing will harm you."* (Luke 10:19) Some snakes are harmless. Some are not. There's a difference between a harmless garden snake and the snake in the garden of Eden. When we encounter temptations, it is sometimes best to run as fast as we can in the opposite direction. Other times, God expects us to fearlessly march into the river of life, snake or no snake, and claim what is rightfully ours.

PONDERINGS

~ When we look at our world, where do we see the results of Satan's deception?

~ Are you more courageous or less courageous than you used to be? What made the difference?

~ Where do you find the courage to march into the river, snake or no snake, and claim what is yours?

O God, strengthen in us the appeal of all that is true and beautiful, that evil may lose its power over us and sin be trampled underneath our feet. Amen.   ~ W. E. Orchard (1877-1955)

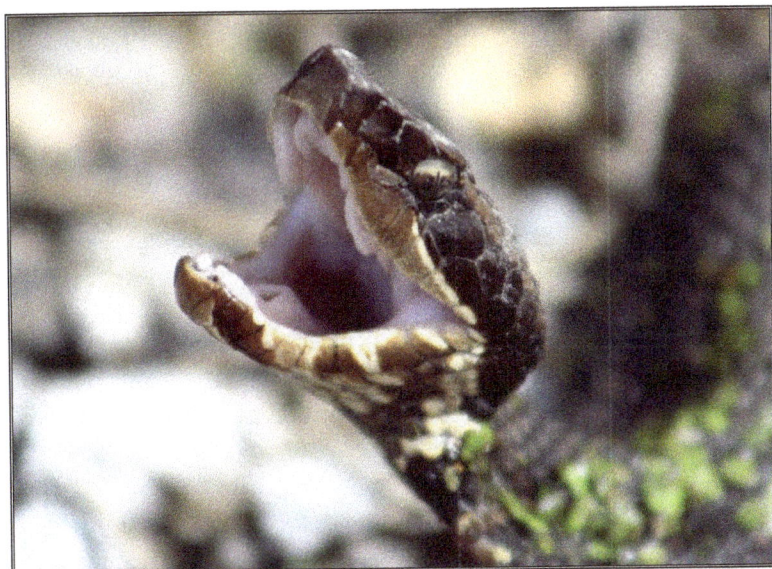

Cottonmouth Snake - Photo by Karin Pelton

Behold, I give to you power
to tread on serpents and scorpions
and over all the power of the enemy:
and nothing shall by any means hurt you.

(Luke 10:19)

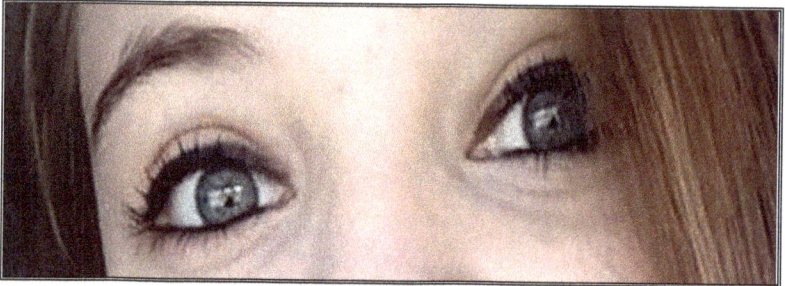

Granddaughter, Destiny Benson

Open my eyes, that I may see
glimpses of truth thou hast for me;
place in my hands the wonderful key
that shall unclasp and set me free.
Silently now I wait for thee,
ready, my God, thy will to see.
Open my eyes, illumine me, Spirit divine!

~ Lyrics by Clara H. Scott (1841-1897)

Idella Pearl
Photos

TOO BLIND TO SEE

We took our family to a piano concert one time performed by Ken Medema, a well-known blind pianist who performs worldwide. He began playing the piano when he was five years old, and three years later began taking lessons in classical music through Braille music instruction. He eventually began performing and recording his own songs and has published 26 albums.

Our son, Bruce, age nine, was sitting up front. Ken Medema turned toward the audience and asked, "How many of you have had piano lessons? If so, let me see your hands!" Our son's hand shot in the air so quickly, it looked as though it were spring loaded. As soon as he realized that his was the only hand in the air and remembered that Ken Medema could see nothing, he sheepishly lowered it, hoping no one would notice. Ken could tell by the audience's reaction that someone had raised their hand, so he enjoyed milking the episode to entertain the audience at Bruce's expense.

I recently read Fanny Crosby's biography by Bernard Ruffin. Born in 1820, Fanny was blind from the age of six weeks old. She was probably the most prolific hymnist in history, writing over 8,000 hymns. She never viewed her blindness as a handicap because she had complete trust in her Savior.

115

Fanny Crosby fully believed that cheerfulness was a choice. In her hymn, Blessed Assurance, written in 1873, she writes:

Perfect submission, all is at rest
I in my Savior am happy and blessed,
Watching and waiting, looking above,
Filled with His goodness, lost in His love.

Fanny Crosby could "see" better than most of us!

In 2 Kings, Chapter 6, Elisha's servant was terrified to see an army with chariots surrounding the city. Elisha prayed for his servant, *"O Lord, open his eyes so he may see."* (vs. 17) God opened the servant's eyes, and he looked and saw the hills full of horses and chariots of fire all around Elisha. Help was there all along, but the servant had limited spiritual eyesight.

Blindness comes in many forms. What we consider blindness may sometimes simply be a stubborn refusal to open our eyes to the truth. We prefer to be blind because, if we don't see the problem, we can ignore our responsibility to fix it.

Are we "too blind to see"? My prayer today is that God will open our eyes to everything God has for us.

PONDERINGS

~ What effect would losing your eyesight have on your life? If you had to give up one of your five senses, which one would it be and why?

~ Read 2 Corinthians 10:5. What does it mean to *"take every thought captive"*? Is attitude really a choice?

~ How limited is my spiritual eyesight? What things might God want me to see that I close my eyes to?

Praise be to you, O LORD; teach me your decrees. Open my eyes that I may see wonderful things in your law. Amen.

~ Psalm 119:12,18

TASTE AND SEE

When we lived in Lusby, Maryland, I took care of two boys: Freddy, age 8, and Andy, age 6. Since their mother was a nurse, they were sometimes at our house on Sundays. One Sunday evening we took them to church for a special program that included a church potluck dinner. My husband and I were in charge of the program and needed to talk briefly with our guest speaker, so we sent the boys through the potluck serving line by themselves. They had never been to a potluck before, so I gave them explicit instructions - just decide which foods were appealing and use the serving spoon to put a little of each on their plates.

My husband and I were standing at the back of the room talking with our guest when I happened to look up and observe the boys going through the food line. To my horror, I saw Andy use the serving spoon to put a small portion of food on his plate (just as I had instructed him) but proceeded to put the spoon into his mouth and lick it off before returning it to the bowl. Although it seemed as though I moved with the speed of lightning, he managed to lick off three serving spoons and return them to their respective bowls before I could reach him.

It was definitely improper etiquette but one thing was for sure – Andy knew what everything tasted like. He knew what was good and what, perhaps, was not. He didn't need to ask anyone else's opinion. He had tasted it for himself.

117

Psalm 34:8 tells us to: *"Taste and see that the Lord is good; blessed is the man who takes refuge in him."* We hear multiple sermons proclaiming the goodness of God, but until we taste for ourselves, we will never know. It's hard to explain to someone what ice-cream tastes like if he or she has never had it. We can describe it, using any number of adjectives, but until we convince them to take a spoonful and put it into their mouths, they will not have a clue.

Have you tasted the goodness of God? It comes in many flavors. Baskin-Robbins is well-known for its "31 flavors" slogan. Anyone can sample a flavor with a small pink spoon. The flavors of God's goodness are so numerous, they are impossible to count. The wonderful part is that God doesn't give us a sample in a little pink plastic spoon. He doesn't tantalize us with nibble-sized blessings of His goodness. He shares abundantly from His storehouse of blessings, and it is never too little.

If we allow God to bless us with His goodness, we will be able to say, *"It is enough!"* God satisfies! All we need to do is "taste and see."

PONDERINGS

~ What are your favorite foods? Do you have a sweet tooth? Why do you think God gave us taste buds?

~ Read Isaiah 55:1-2. Why does God frequently use food to represent His kingdom?

~ Read Matthew 5:13. In what ways can we be "flavor" to the world?

O Living Bread from heaven, how well You feed Your guest! The gifts that You have given, have filled my heart with rest. Oh, wondrous food of blessing, Oh, cup that heals our woes! My heart, this gift possessing, with praises overflows. Amen.
~ Lyrics by Johann von Rist (1607-1667)

WHERE'S THE POWER?

In the 1980's, I worked for Leaseway Transportation as the first shift supervisor of the Data Processing Center. One Thursday night, I received a call at midnight from the Comptroller of the company. Evidently, the third shift employees all called in sick and the Comptroller decided he would go in and print the payroll checks to meet the Friday deadline. The only problem was that he had never done it before and could not get the printer to work. I did not relish the thought of getting dressed and going in to work and, since it was a relatively simple procedure, I decided I could talk him through it over the phone.

I spent the next 45 minutes telling him how to access the computer files, which buttons to push and how to line up the checks in the printer. He still could not get the checks to print. It finally dawned on me that I had not told him to press the "on" button, assuming he had already done so. What a difference it makes when we connect to the power source to complete the circuit!

Many of the struggles and challenges we experience in life stem from our ignorance on how to properly complete our spiritual circuit. We come to church or Bible Study and learn new ways to walk closer to our Lord – and that's a good thing. But then we charge forward thinking we now have the proper knowledge and the right formulas that will guarantee our spiritual growth. We neglect to stay connected to the Source. Have you ever tried to explain something to someone only to be quickly interrupted with, *"Yes, I know!"*? That's what we do to God. He has so much more to say, but we cut Him off before we have fully received all He wants to impart.

The power button was not hidden nor out of the Comptroller's reach. It was nearby, completely accessible. He could have used one finger and pressed it at any time. It was simply not part of his perceived solution and was overlooked. God, also, is not hidden from us nor is He out of our reach. He is only a prayer away, and He makes His Word accessible. *"Now what I am commanding you today is not too difficult for you or beyond your reach. No, the word is very near you; it is in your mouth and in your heart so you may obey it."* (Deuteronomy 30:11, 14)

Through God's Word and prayer, we can reach out and touch Him at any time. The incomprehensible part is when we overlook Him as the Ultimate Solution. Whether we lack persistence, courage, faith, self-control, self-confidence, wisdom or companionship, He is the Ultimate Provider. Pressing our spiritual "on" button means saying "yes" to the Father. Completing our spiritual circuit means becoming "one" with the Father and with His purpose.

PONDERINGS

~ Which of my self-absorbed tendencies tend to create breaks in my spiritual line?

~ Read 1 Corinthians 1:9. What does it mean to you that we are allowed to have fellowship with the Son of God? Share about a time when you felt most connected with God?

~ What works best for you as a spiritual battery charger?

O my Father, You know I always delight to commune with You in my lone and silent heart; I am never full of You; I am never weary of You; I am always desiring You. I hunger with strong hope and affection for You, and I thirst for Your grace and spirit. Amen.
~ Ralph Waldo Emerson (1803-1882)

Judy Billingsley

SERVICE WITH A SMILE

Every Thursday is Senior Citizens' Day at Kroger's. Since they offer seniors a 5% discount, the grocery aisles are always filled to the max with elderly shoppers. In addition to saving money, seniors also have an added blessing. Volunteers faithfully appear at Kroger's each Thursday to assist seniors where needed. They sanitize grocery carts, help locate hard-to-find items, unload groceries onto the checkout counter and load purchased groceries into the car.

The volunteers wear bright lime-green t-shirts with the name "A.C.T.S." (Acknowledging Christ Through Service.) "A.C.T.S." is the brainstorm of Tracy Harlan, Children's Pastor of First Church of God in Marion, IL. She explained to me that God inspired her through an evangelist at camp who emphasized the need to go outside the walls of the church to "show them Jesus."

Each month, several members of First Church of God set aside the many responsibilities and obligations of their own lives for the purpose of sharing their time and energy with others to "show them Jesus." And...they do it with a smile! The smile comes easily because they are not serving out of obligation, but from the heart. It is a smile that reflects the love of Jesus for every person God created.

We, too, are called to "show them Jesus!" We are called to "Acknowledge Christ Through Service." Jesus tells us in Matthew 25:40: *"...I tell you the truth, whatever you did for one of the least of these brothers of mine, you did for me."*

I joined a small group one time called "The Mayberry Bible Study." It helped us search for gospel truths in the Andy Griffith television series. Where can a television show be found today that is so family friendly and includes a moral lesson in every episode? Lesson One in the book zeroed in on the "heavenly purpose of earthly service." We observed many practical examples of a small town sheriff who consistently put the needs of his community above his own. Andy Griffith gave "service with a smile."

The Bible is clear: *"If anyone has material possessions and sees his brother in need but has no pity on him, how can the love of God be in him? Dear children, let us not love with words or tongue but with actions and in truth."* (1 John 3:17, 18) And, do it with a smile!

PONDERINGS

~ In what ways can a bad attitude be a pothole in the road to your chosen destination?

~ Read John 13:1-17. Do you think Jesus had a smile on his face while washing feet? Have you ever served out of duty rather than desire? How hard is it to be joyful during these times?

~ What is the heavenly purpose of earthly service?

Lord, Open my eyes to the needs of others for this is the service you have chosen - to loose the chains of injustice, set the oppressed free, share my food with the hungry, provide for the poor and clothe the naked. Then my light will break forth like the dawn and your glory will be my rear guard. Amen. ~ Based on Isaiah 58:6-8

THE DEFUSER

When my husband, Jack, encounters a grouchy salesperson, he takes it on as a personal challenge to get him or her to smile before we leave the store. Since he can be quite witty, he is usually successful. There is one clerk in a small store who always seems to be moody. We now find him chatting amiably with us every time we come. I'd like to think that a large amount of the credit is due to my husband's efforts.

Our world has an overabundance of grouchy people. I'd rather not include myself in that statistic, because I can usually see the bright side of things. One day, however, I found myself growing grouchier by the minute in the saga of buying a new upright vacuum cleaner. We found one we liked but it came with expensive cloth filter bags. We told the salesman we wanted to buy this particular vacuum cleaner only if paper replacement bags were available. He assured us they were and sold us a set of paper bags with the vacuum. But a couple weeks later when we tried to change the bag, we discovered they were designed for a canister vacuum cleaner.

No problem. We would just go back to the store (trip #2) and exchange them. When we arrived, we were told by a different salesman that the cloth replacement bags were the only ones available for that vacuum cleaner. We were not convinced so we returned home and called the factory. The factory gave us the code number for the replacement bags. So we went back to the store (trip #3) only to find out that the factory had given us the code number for the cloth bag. A 3rd salesman reaffirmed there were no paper bags available.

We went home and put the vacuum cleaner in the trunk intending to return it. We marched back to the store (trip # 4), ready to talk with a manager and demand the right to return the vacuum. But salesman #4 promised he could be of help. He was so gentle, so compassionate, so kind and so reassuring that all our anxiety was quickly defused. He gave us paper bags that fit (with a smile) at no extra charge. My irritation drained away like dirty water down a bathtub drain.

There are many things in this life that hit us right between the eyes. How many times do we allow our circumstances to dictate our attitude? God is our Defuser. He is SO gentle, SO compassionate, SO kind and SO reassuring, that all our anxiety quickly melts in the warmth of His love. 1 Peter 5:7 tells us to... *"Cast all your anxiety on him because he cares for you."* We have no excuse to be grouchy, because God is The Great Defuser of everything contrary to His Kingdom.

PONDERINGS

~ What makes you grouchy? What works best to defuse your anger?

~ List ways you can be a "defuser," overcoming evil with good?

~ Read Ephesians 4:26-27. Is it ever alright to be angry?

O Lord God Almighty, redeem my soul from its bondage that I may be free to live henceforth, not for myself, but for You. Help me to put away self, and to remember that this life is not given for my ease, my enjoyment. It is a schooling time for the eternal home You have prepared for those who love you. Amen.

~ Maria Hare (1798-1870)

MONKEYS IN MY LIVING ROOM

Whenever my husband received a job transfer that included relocation to another state, he would go on ahead of the family to purchase the new house while I stayed behind to sell the old one. He always did an excellent job of choosing houses that pleased me. We normally liked many of the same things in houses except for one. My husband is extremely conservative by nature and I delight in color and contrast. The house in Oklahoma he picked out had beige carpeting throughout and matching draperies of dusty green in every room. It was actually very becoming, but the longer we were there, the more I began to crave a splash of color.

When it came time for retirement, after much internet research, we chose Marion, Illinois as our new place of residence. Since my husband purchased all the other houses, he said it was my turn. I was thrilled. He stayed behind with my mother while I drove from Oklahoma to Southern Illinois by myself. I found a lovely three-bedroom villa that would meet our needs. I immediately fell in love with the bright yellow kitchen and saw numerous decorating possibilities for the rest of the house. After we moved in, my first project was to purchase an area rug for the laminate floors in the living room. It didn't take long at Home Depot to find exactly what I wanted – a red rug with designs that included leopards and monkeys. I added bright red swag curtains to the windows for just the right touch. I am thoroughly enjoying the splashes of color in our home, and I love having monkeys in my living room.

Do you have any monkeys in your living room? Chances are, you prefer beige carpeting and that's okay but, to be honest, many of us have settled into a beige, dusty-green mediocre existence. Each morning, as we go through the same motions as the day before, we begin to long for a splash of color in our lives.

One of my favorite passages of scripture is found in Ezekiel, Chapter 47. I love the visual image of a great river flowing from the throne of God. The Bible tells us that as the river enters stagnant waters, the sea becomes fresh. Verse 9 says, *"where the river flows, everything will live."* The river represents the flow of the Holy Spirit in us. John 7:38 (NKJV) says: *"He who believes in Me, as the Scripture has said, out of his heart will flow rivers of living water."* There is NOTHING mediocre about living water!

It is not mandatory to have monkeys in our living rooms, but it is essential to allow the Spirit to flow through us, filling us with life. *"Where the river flows, everything will live!"*

PONDERINGS

~ What type of personality are you? Do you dread changes or crave something new? How do you know it's time for a change?

~ What adjective would you use to describe your relationship with God? Stale? Vibrant? Healthy? Sporadic? Satisfying?

~ Read Isaiah 44:3. Why do you think God uses water to describe the Holy Spirit?

Heavenly Father, Sovereign Lord, by Your glorious Name adored!
Streams of grace our thirst repress, starting from the wilderness;
Still we gasp Your grace to know, here forever let it flow,
Make the thirsty land a pool; fix the Spirit in our soul. Amen.
~ Lyrics by Charles Wesley (1707 - 1788)

Photo by James Andersen

LIFE PACKS A PUNCH!

I was reading a while back about Mantis Shrimp. Although they are only a few inches long, they can throw the fastest and strongest punch of any animal. They strike with the force of a rifle bullet and can even shatter aquarium glass. Mantis Shrimp use an ingenious energy storage system. When the arm is cocked, a ratchet holds it in place, then the muscles contract and build up energy. When the latch is released, all the energy is released at once, acting like a spring and accelerating up to 10,000 times the force of gravity. It really "packs a punch."

Life can be like that sometimes. Everything is going well. Life is predictable, satisfactory and rewarding. Then, when we least expect it, "life packs a punch," turning our world upside down.

That's the way I felt on March 1, 2010, when my world came to an abrupt halt in an automobile accident. My husband and I were on our way to a home-based Bible Study group north of the highway. Our view was blocked, and my husband unknowingly turned in front of an oncoming Dodge Ram pickup. Paramedics were at the scene quickly, called by Good Samaritan witnesses. The fire department was called to extricate us from our car.

My husband was taken to Heartland Regional Medical Center in Marion, IL, and I was airlifted to Deaconess Hospital in Evansville, IN, which is a Level 1 Trauma Center. My husband was treated and released the next day. He had a large gash on the head and damaged back muscles. After nine days in the trauma unit, I was transferred to Shawnee Christian Nursing Center in Herrin, IL for rehabilitation. In addition to 19 stitches in the forehead, I had a broken collarbone, multiple broken ribs, a lacerated liver, a punctured lung and colorful bruises from head to toe. My recovery was a lengthy one, but I am blessed!

Romans 8:28 tells us, *"We know that in all things God works for the good of those who love him, who have been called according to his purpose."* If there is one thing I have learned from this experience, it is that God is not done with me yet. In His great mercy, an accident that should have taken my life or at the very least, left me incapacitated, has instead given me a new lease on life, a renewed appreciation for every opportunity, and the sense of the privilege that is mine for serving the awesome God of the universe. That really "packs a punch!"

PONDERINGS

~ What is the biggest challenge facing you today? In what ways are you tempted to feel that your circumstances are beyond God's power?

~ Read John 11:34-44. What was Jesus' response to the evil of Lazarus' death? What does that teach us?

~ If you were God, would you have designed the world differently? Would you remove all suffering and evil? What do you think would be the result?

O Lord, Help us to trust You when we cannot trace Your hand, assured that You do all things well, and that all things work together for good to those who love You. Amen.

~ 1789 Book of Common Prayer

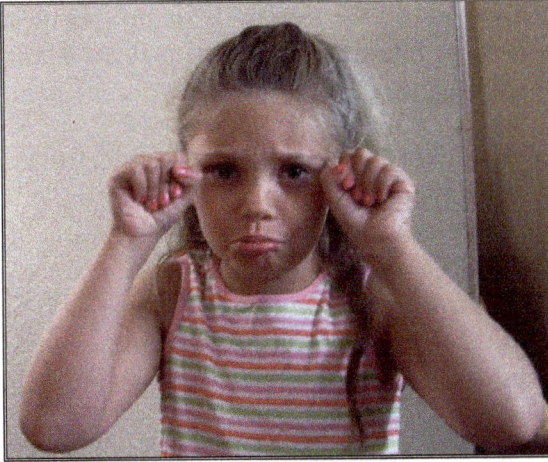
Granddaughter, Destiny Benson

FRUSTRATED

Have you ever been frustrated? Chances are, the answer is "yes". Being frustrated can mean many things - disappointment, dissatisfaction and disillusionment. Allowing ourselves to be frustrated can zap our energy and easily sidetrack us from our goals.

Frustrations in life frequently express themselves in dreams. Many years ago, as a new college student, I had a recurring dream that I was trying to get to my first day of class. I remember taking elevators that went nowhere. One elevator even took me up several stories and opened onto the roof. Once, I found myself in a long hallway of rooms where every room had the same room number, but it was not the number I was looking for. I continually looked at my watch thinking, *"Time is running out. I have to get to class before it starts."*

My husband had a dream one night that he was in a play and forgot his lines. He faked it through the first act and then refused to go on stage for the second. He was happy to wake up and discover it was all a dream. Being frustrated can leave us with a sense of urgency such as my dream about getting to class on time did. Or, as in my husband's dream, when our frustrations are caused by our own mistakes or inadequacies, we simply give up. How many times have we been so frustrated that we wish it were a dream and we could wake up and find it gone?

In the book of Ezra, God's people had returned from captivity in Babylon and were attempting to rebuild the temple. But *"the peoples around them set out to discourage the people of Judah and make them afraid to go on building. They hired counselors to work against them and frustrate their plans..."* (Ezra 4:4-5) Satan knows that allowing a little frustration to creep into our lives works best of all, and mental frustrations can be worse than physical ones.

But God never leaves us hopeless and helpless! His answer to our frustrations is found in Psalm 37:4-6. *"Delight yourself in the LORD, and He shall give you the desires of your heart. Commit your way to the LORD, trust also in Him, and He shall bring it to pass. He shall bring forth your righteousness as the light, and your justice as the noonday."* (NKJV)

Step number one is to *"delight yourself in the Lord."* Steps two and three are to *"commit your way to the Lord"* and *"trust in Him."* God has the power to convert our worst frustrations into our best victories!

PONDERINGS

~ What frustrates you the most? Do your worst frustrations usually have to do with things or other people or yourself?

~ Read Psalm 37:1-2. Do you get frustrated at injustice? Fretting is an inward emotion. How should we deal with injustice?

~ How are frustration and faith opposites?

Father, let me not grow weary of doing good, for in due season I will reap if I do not give up. Help me to throw off everything that hinders and the sin that so easily entangles and run with perseverance the race marked out for me. Amen.
~ based on Galatians 6:9 & Hebrews 12:1

130

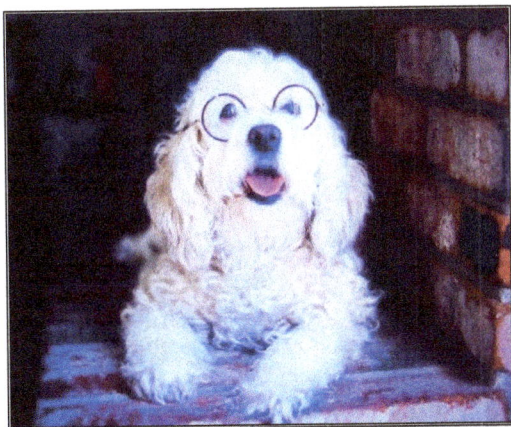

Ginger

WELCOME!

In the winter of 1977, my husband, Jack, moved to an apartment in Chicago to start his new job and I stayed behind in Lusby, Maryland to sell our home. When it came time for the house closing, I obtained power of attorney for my husband's signature because he was on a business trip to the United Arab Emirates. After the moving van was loaded, our two daughters, Rhonda and Kerry, and our white Cockapoo, Ginger, started the 750-mile trip with me to our new home.

We made plans to stay at a hotel one night on the way. I had dutifully called ahead to ask if they allowed dogs. They told me, "No problem!" But when we arrived, I discovered that they had placed us on the third floor. I reminded them that we had requested the first floor because of the dog. The hotel clerk immediately shushed me, with a look of horror, said, "Because of the what?!" Evidently dogs were not allowed after all and we had been misinformed.

The clerk relented and allowed us to stay the night, giving us a first-floor room, but admonished us to "keep the dog out of sight!" Hmmm. How do you take a dog that needs to go outside, down a long hallway on a leash, past a multitude of occupied rooms and keep her out of sight? So we devised a plan.

I would go outside first, one of my daughters would hand Ginger out the hotel window, and then, when she was done, I would hand her back in through the window. Although I had to step over large snow banks, the plan worked perfectly.

We had to sneak our dog in and out of the room because Ginger was not a welcome guest. There are times when we do not feel like a welcome guest in God's presence either. We come to Him in prayer but, because of our failures and imperfections, we do not feel worthy enough to feel comfortable in His presence.

When we are the least worthy, however, God throws out His extravagant Welcome Mat. He bids us come and share in His holiness when we have none of our own. We don't need to sneak in or out of a window or use the back door to find God. We can come boldly to His throne. When we have messed up for the umpteenth time…when we have used up our last excuse…our loving God throws His arms around us and makes us feel welcome.

We, in turn, are encouraged to welcome others. Romans 15:7 tells us, *"Therefore welcome one another as Christ has welcomed you, for the glory of God."* Welcome to the Kingdom of God.

PONDERINGS

~ Have you ever gone somewhere where you did not feel welcome? How can we make others feel more welcome at church?

~ How does our guilt prevent us from feeling welcome in God's presence?

~ Read Hebrews 4:16. What does it mean to come "boldly" to the throne of grace? Why is it called a throne of "grace"?

As we come into this place of prayer, out of darkness into light, we come, O God, to You; from all falsehood and unreality, to truth, to certainty, to the welcome of Your arms and the shining of Your face. Amen.   ~ W. E. Orchard (1877-1955)

Danielle Barter

FINISH THE RACE

My friend, Danielle Barter, is a jogger. She recently had an interesting experience during her jog and shares this story:

> Today, I jogged with a goat. It saw me, ran straight for me (I thought it was going to head-butt me), then fell in beside me for a full mile, panting and bleating loudly. (Perhaps it sensed I could communicate with it since I had kissed another goat at the high school a few months ago for the FFA fundraiser.) We created quite a spectacle for the fleet of workers leaving their boss's farm. Every man among them was laughing - hard. Even funnier is the fact that one after one, the drivers of the fleet of vehicles who passed me would roll down their windows, and between belly-laughs, say, *"You're jogging with a goat!"* As if I hadn't already noticed!

> I felt bad leaving the goat behind when it could no longer keep up. That goat really needed some exercise. It was quite chunky. If it hadn't invested so much of its energy in bleating the whole time we ran, it might have been able to complete the full four miles with me, instead of giving up after one.

Danielle's "goat story" gives us cause to wonder. Where do WE expend our energy? When we choose our goal, do we use all our energy bleating and complaining about how difficult the task is?

Do we use every ounce of our strength on pity parties, thinking about how unfair it is that others seem to be able to achieve success without the sacrifices we have to make? For some of us, our "get-up-and-go" seems to have "got-up-and-went." Perhaps it is because we have allowed our energy to be used up on nonessential things.

Some of the Israelites in the Bible, (like Danielle's goat) put a great deal of energy into complaining. *"The rabble with them began to crave other food, and again the Israelites started wailing and said, 'If only we had meat to eat! We remember the fish we ate in Egypt at no cost - also the cucumbers, melons, leeks, onions and garlic. But now we have lost our appetite; we never see anything but this manna!'"* (Numbers 11:4-6) The Lord had been good to them when they had nothing to eat, providing free food in the form of manna. Yet they channeled their energy into negativity. Perhaps that's why they wandered in the desert for 40 years instead of reaching the Promised Land.

If we choose to invest our energy into whining and bleating, we will never complete the race God has set before us. Victory is ours when we stop complaining and use our strength to "finish the race!"

PONDERINGS

~ Read Philippians 2:14-16. Is it possible to do "all" things without complaining? What type of things tend to trigger your whine button?

~ Do you enjoy being in the company of a "complainer"? Why or why not?

~ What is the difference between complaining and constructive criticism? Explain.

Lord, may I be able to say, along with the Apostle Paul... *"I have fought the good fight, I have finished the race, I have kept the faith."* Amen. ~ based on 2 Timothy 4:7

Grandson, Zac Benson

HUNGRY?

Our grandson, Zac, enjoys his pancakes. What are YOU hungry for? My daughter, Rhonda, shares the following:

MONDAY: Made a huge pot of homemade Ham and Bean soup with the Thanksgiving ham bone from the freezer. The soup burned a little, so it had that distinctive "charcoal" taste. Served with spoons and crackers.

TUESDAY: Leftover Ham and Bean soup. Decided to try cornmeal dumplings in it. I got the soup bubbling, then dropped the cornmeal batter into it. The batter disintegrated and mixed into the soup. I left the soup alone to bubble, thicken and burn underneath the dumplings adding to that distinctive burnt flavor. The soup was now Ham and Bean Cornmeal Mush, worthy of a fork.

WEDNESDAY: Took some hamburger from the freezer for meatloaf. Mixed a generous portion of Ham and Bean Cornmeal Mush into the meat along with some eggs and breadcrumbs. Shaped it into a pretty meatloaf. The soup was now Ham and Bean Cornmeal Mush Meatloaf with a distinctive burnt flavor.

THURSDAY: Took out some nice Tilapia from the freezer.

Decided not to get creative with the fish and just baked it. Took another generous portion of Ham and Bean Cornmeal Mush, added the basic ingredients of cornbread, plopped it into a pan and stuck it in the oven. The soup was now Ham and Bean Mush Cornbread and, even though it was as dense as a brick, it was somewhat tasty even with that distinctive burnt flavor.

FRIDAY: Threw out the remaining Ham and Bean Cornmeal Mush, the Mush Meatloaf and the Mush Cornbread brick. After all, it's pizza night!

It's admirable to be persistent, but there comes a time when we should give up and go a different direction. It's possible to be very tenacious about the wrong things. We look to television to eliminate our boredom. We look to excess food to satisfy our spiritual hunger. Enough is enough. Some things are good in moderation, but they are not meant to satisfy our hunger for God.

The time has come to throw out what is not working and latch onto what does work. Are you hungry? Jesus told us in Matthew 5:6, *"Blessed are those who hunger and thirst for righteousness, for they will be filled."*

PONDERINGS

~ What's your favorite food? What's the hungriest you have ever been? What did it feel like?

~ Have you ever spoiled your appetite before a meal? What things might spoil your appetite for righteousness?

~ Read Matthew 6:33. Righteousness means being "right" with God? How does your happiness depend on that relationship?

Lord Jesus, grant that my soul may hunger after You, the Bread of Angels, having all sweetness and savor and every delightful taste. May my heart ever hunger after You, and may my inmost soul be filled with the sweetness of Your savor. Amen.
~ St. Bonaventure of Bagnoregio (1221-1274)

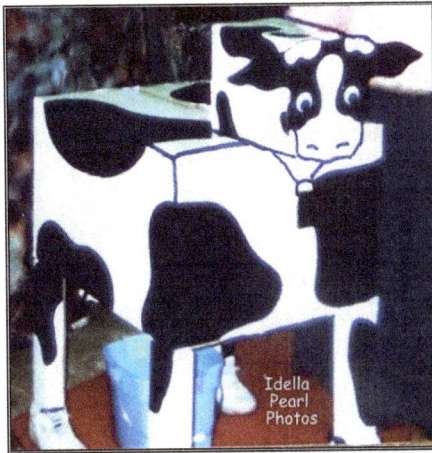

Idella Pearl Photos

FINDING A TREASURE

The expression, *"One man's trash is another man's treasure,"* could very well apply to garage sales. You can find a lot of unusual things at garage sales. Believe it or not, my husband and I saw a coffin at a garage sale in Clarendon Hills, Illinois one time. (I didn't ask if it was used.) I even sold a "cow" at one of my garage sales. Our church in Mustang, Oklahoma was having a program with a cowboy theme. My husband and I took a black and white Gateway computer box and made an adorable black and white square cow to use as part of the decorations, complete with gym shoes and a bucket underneath. We wondered what to do with our square cow afterwards and decided to put it in our garage sale. We asked the gentleman who bought it for $3.00 what in the world he planned to do with it. His reply?..... *"I'm going to put it on my neighbor's porch, ring the doorbell and run!"*

It's surprising how many people go to garage sales and find something they consider valuable or desirable from other people's castaways. I love going to garage sales. My husband is of the opinion that all garage sales are full of useless junk, but I find them both a source of entertainment and an opportunity to find a great bargain. We do have to be careful we are not spending our hard-earned cash for something worthless. A bargain is not a bargain if we don't need it or if the quality is questionable.

Psalm 119:37 gives us some good advice, *"Turn my eyes away from worthless things..."* There are a lot of worthless things in this world. We must constantly evaluate whether we are placing too much emphasis on the worthless things of life and giving little thought to things that truly matter.

When we lived in Las Vegas, my mother accidentally put her original engagement ring in our garage sale. Fortunately my daughter spotted it before the sale started and removed it. Someone could have found a treasure. Sometimes we find our treasures in unlikely places.

God placed a treasure in an unlikely place as well. Although we are unworthy, He gave us His Holy Spirit to live inside us. The Apostle Paul says it this way, " *...we have this treasure in jars of clay to show that this all-surpassing power is from God and not from us."* (2 Corinthians 4:7)

And what a treasure that is!

PONDERINGS

~ Read Luke 12:33-34. What is the relationship between earthly treasure and worry? How does it help to share your treasures?

~ What do you consider your best earthly treasures? Are they tangible or intangible?

~ Read Matthew 6:19. What are some of the warning signs that we are building up "earthly" treasures instead of "heavenly" ones?

Jesus, priceless treasure, source of purest pleasure, Friend most sure and true. Long my heart was burning, fainting much and yearning, thirsting, Lord, for You. Yours I am, O spotless Lamb, so will I let nothing hide You, seek no joy beside You! Amen.
~ Lyrics by Catherine Winkworth (1827-1878)

Painting by Francisco Goya, 1806

SPITTING NAILS

While I was at the hospital waiting to get an MRI, I saw a surly-looking prisoner in an orange suit being led down the hallway. He was in shackles and chains and accompanied by a big guard, complete with gun. I won't quickly forget the look on the prisoner's face that said, *"I may be subdued for now, but if I get half a chance, watch out!"* My mind played the scenario. MRI's are magnetic. If the prisoner needs an MRI, they must first remove the metal restraints. I was suddenly grateful for the powerful-looking guard. His job was to protect us should the prisoner decide to suddenly vent his anger on anyone within reach.

Do you ever feel like venting your anger? What makes you mad? What brings you to the boiling point? What (or who) has the ability to pull your trigger and make you spit nails? We occasionally succumb to inward or outward explosions of anger for various reasons. Stop lights? Not getting invited to a party? Someone lies to us? Noisy neighbors at 3 AM? False accusations? Unruly children? Criminals that prey on the weak? Someone puts a scratch on our new car?

Is anger wrong? The Bible tells us, "...*Do not let the sun go down while you are still angry.*" (Ephesians 4:26) On the other hand,

Jesus became angry enough in the temple to overturn the tables of the money changers who were buying and selling in God's house. (Matthew 21:12) There is a time and a place for anger.

We should be angry with Satan. He has bossed us around far too long. He approaches us like a big bully and says, *"Give me your integrity. Give me your goals and dreams. Give me your wisdom. Give me your peace."* At times, we are tempted to give up without a fight. He is pushing us around, and we are allowing it. Satan attempts to kill our self-esteem and fill us with unnecessary guilt. He especially tries to devour our faith in the Almighty God of the Universe. Let's not hand our lives over to him on a silver platter without a fight! Ephesians 6:10-11 in the Message Bible says, *"God is strong, and he wants you strong. So take everything the Master has set out for you, well-made weapons of the best materials. And put them to use so you will be able to stand up to everything the Devil throws your way."*

Satan is portrayed as an ominous, undefeatable adversary. But Jesus is our Security Guard, and if we trust in Jesus, Satan's hands are tied. *"We are more than conquerors through him who loved us!"* (Romans 8:37)

PONDERINGS

~ What makes you angry? Why? When is anger healthy, and when is it harmful and unproductive?

~ Which of your dreams has Satan stolen? Are you ready for a fight? What is the best way to defeat Satan?

~ How much confidence do you have in Jesus as your Security Guard? When is it best to let Him do the fighting for you?

O Father, your power is greater than all powers.
O Son, under your leadership we cannot fear anything.
O Spirit, under your protection there is nothing we cannot
   overcome. Amen.   ~ A prayer of the Kikuyu, Kenya

Joe, Sam and Ezra at the Airport

COVER ALL YOUR BASES

On July 14, 2009, we drove to St. Louis, Missouri to pick up our two teenage grandsons, Sam and Joe and their friend, Ezra. They were flying from Oklahoma City to spend two weeks with us in Marion, Illinois. On our way to the airport, we noticed police cars with flashing lights blocking every entrance ramp to the freeway. I facetiously remarked to my husband, *"Wow. The President must be coming!"* It immediately dawned on us that, yes indeed, the President WAS coming. President Barak Obama was scheduled to throw out the first ball at Busch Stadium for the All-Star game.

After a lengthy wait at the airport, we welcomed the teenagers. As we left the airport heading toward home, we once again observed multiple police cars with flashing lights, blocking all entrance ramps. Soon after, we passed the Presidential motorcade on the opposite side of the freeway. At least a dozen police cars, as well as motorcycles with lights flashing and sirens blaring, surrounded the limousine. It was quite a sight. They were taking every precaution to protect our President, covering all their bases.

If the police knew the direction from which the enemy might come, it would have simplified things, but enemies never publicly announce their coming. They count on the element of surprise.

141

Our enemy is Satan. He relies on the element of surprise as well. If we knew which direction Satan would be coming from to temp us, we would need to guard only one entrance into our hearts and minds and souls. But he is noted for his deception. In fact, in Revelation 12:9, he is called, *"the deceiver of the whole world."* Therefore, we need to "cover all our bases."

In the book of Nehemiah, God's people were attempting to rebuild the walls of Jerusalem. When their enemies heard about it, they threatened to fight against them. God's people not only prayed, but also took action. *"We countered with prayer to our God and set a round-the-clock guard against them.....They stationed armed guards at the most vulnerable places and assigned people by families with their swords, lances and bows."* (Nehemiah 4:9 & 13) They were ready! They covered all their bases.

Which entrance to our heart and soul is the most insecure? We must choose our heaviest guard at the entrances where we are most vulnerable, whether it be pride, envy, anger, laziness, pleasure-seeking or even a pity party.

Don't hold back on the power! Use a prayer of faith to our God first and foremost. Then use the flashing lights and sirens of the Word of God and the Name of Jesus. We must let the enemy know we mean business. Let's cover ALL our bases!

PONDERINGS

~ Read Philippians 4:8. How is our thought life connected to our vulnerability?

~ Read Ephesians 6:16. What part does faith play in our fight against Satan?

~ What is the difference between contentment and complacency? What symptoms of complacency do you see in your life?

Lord, we beseech You to continue Your gracious protection to us. Defend us from all dangers and mischiefs, and from the fear of them. Amen.   ~ 1789 U. S. Book of Common Prayer

Jack and Idella ("Selfie" - 1959)

HEART OF A SERVANT

My husband, Jack, has a servant's heart. It was probably instilled in him from a young age by the example of his father, George Edwards. George owned and operated a small grocery store in Newberry, Michigan. No one in town ever had to go hungry. They could always come to his store and get a bag of groceries whether they had money or not. Even if they came to the house after hours, George would go to the store to get them some food. He also invested himself in many other service projects such as organizing the Lion's Club Christmas party for underprivileged children.

When we lived in Oklahoma City, my husband and I helped our church sponsor meals for the homeless through Skyline Ministries. Some of the people who came were from the nearby low-income neighborhood, and some were actually homeless. There was a church service first, and then we put food on tables at the back of the church. Everyone went through the serving line to get a large plateful of home-cooked food...everyone, that is, except Cheryl. She was not permitted to go through the line because of her offensive odor. Cheryl had seeping sores all over her legs and ankles, wore men's tennis shoes two sizes too big and wore every layer of clothes she owned, one on top of the other. There was always a large black gob of goo hanging from her hair that looked like bear grease. Cheryl was a "bag lady" in the true sense of the word. In fact, as soon as she arrived, the director headed up and down the aisles spraying a can of Lysol.

Cheryl sat by herself in a corner of the church, and one of us had to fix her a plate and hand-deliver it. My husband always volunteered. In fact, he would stay and chat for a while. At first she was belligerent, grabbing the food and asking him to leave. But little by little he won her confidence and she began to appreciate his efforts to help.

Jesus told His disciples in Mark 9:35, *"If anyone wants to be first, he must be the very last, and the servant of all."* Being a servant may mean sacrificing our own desires for the good of others.

Another important element of true service is that it begins with a servant's heart, serving out of love rather than duty - serving willingly, wholeheartedly and without reservation. Mother Teresa (1910-1997) said, *"Prayer in action is love, and love in action is service."* It brings joy to our Heavenly Father when we have the "heart of a servant!"

PONDERINGS

~ Has anyone made an impact on your life by serving you?

~ Leo Buscaglia (1924-1998) said, *"It's not enough to have lived. We should be determined to live for something. May I suggest that it be creating joy for others, sharing what we have, bringing hope to the lost and love to the lonely."* How important is this to you?

~ Read Ephesians 6:18. How is prayer a way of serving others?

Father, You have taught us that whenever we feed the hungry or welcome a stranger or visit the sick, we have done it unto You. You also taught us that it is more blessed to give than to receive. Give us, O Lord, the heart of a servant. Amen.

(Based on Matthew 25:40 and Acts 20:35)

Mrs. Malaprop
Character in a production of the play,
"The Rivals" by R.B. Sheridan (1751-1816)

WHAT DID YOU SAY?

In 1988, one of my co-workers at Leaseway Transportation in Downers Grove, Illinois, had a habit of consistently misusing words. Her speech displayed classic examples of malapropism, which is a humorous misuse of the English language, using words that sound similar to the correct one but ridiculously wrong in context. The word "malapropism" is based on a character in a play, Mrs. Malaprop (R.B. Sheridan's comedy, THE RIVALS), who was noted for her misuse of words. My co-worker would say things such as, "neon stockings" instead of "nylon stockings," "fire distinguisher" instead of "fire extinguisher", or "it's just a pigment of your imagination" instead of "a figment of your imagination."

She always took me by surprise. It would take me a moment to realize she had used the wrong word. I never corrected her nor let her know how humorous it was. I always wished that I had written them all down because they were delightfully entertaining.

We misuse words as well, but some words we misuse are not as humorous. We sometimes say "yes" when we should say "no." Titus 2:11-12 tells us, *"For the grace of God...teaches us to say 'No' to ungodliness and worldly passions, and to live self-*

145

controlled, upright and godly lives in this present age." Many times, we say "no" when we should say "yes." Jesus asked Peter in John 21:15, *"...do you truly love me more than these?"* There are times we say "can't" instead of "can." Philippians 4:13 tells us, *"I can do everything through him who gives me strength."* We may say "tomorrow" when we should say "today." *"For as long as it's still God's today, keep each other on your toes so sin doesn't slow down your reflexes."* (Hebrews 3:13)

It is also possible that we say "mine" when we should say "yours." 1 Corinthians 6:19 says, *"Do you not know that your body is a temple of the Holy Spirit, who is in you, whom you have received from God? You are not your own."* We belong to God.

We would be wise to choose our words carefully and be cautious of the constant inner dialogue we hold within ourselves. They can be statements of criticism or praise, truth or lies, doubt or faith. Every word matters! Words can change our lives. *"May the words of my mouth and the meditation of my heart be pleasing in your sight, O Lord, my Rock and my Redeemer."* (Psalm 19:14)

What did you say?

PONDERINGS

~ There's an old saying, *"Sticks and stones may break my bones, but words will never hurt me."* Is this true? Why or why not?

~ Read Proverbs 18:21. What does it mean when it says that death and life are in the power of the tongue?

~ Read Exodus 20:7. How does this verse demonstrate the importance of words?

Enable us, Lord, to reach the end of our lives in peace, forsaking all idle words, acting virtuously, shunning our passions, and raising ourselves above the things of this world. Amen.
~ *A Syriac liturgy (early fourth century)*

146

"I hope I glow!" Sarah Martin

VIBRANT RELATIONSHIPS

This is my buddy, Sarah. It may seem strange that I am 77 and Sarah is only 30, and yet we are good friends. We have what I call a vibrant relationship. One definition for "vibrant" is bright, spirited and strong.

I was in a discussion group one time at church that talked about vibrant spirituality. The leader asked the question, *"What color are you spiritually?"* One participant said she was definitely blue, representing depression, because of all the recent failures in her life. Another said her spirit was yellow, representing sunshine and the warmth of God's love and forgiveness. Another said she was plaid, because she was a little bit of everything, but having difficulty finding God's perfect will for her life.

Sarah was a young teen at the time and loved vibrant colors. So when I asked her what color she was spiritually, she said her spirit was green to represent spiritual growth, but that she was a *"neon-green wannabe."* She said, *"I hope I glow!"* In other words, she wanted to glow with spiritual health.

When our son, Bruce, was four months old, I took him to the pediatrician for a check-up. The doctor looked me in the eye and said, *"Your son doesn't like his green veggies, does he!"* It surprised me that the color of my baby's skin would reveal his preference for creamed carrots and squash over green beans and spinach!

If the food that goes inside us affects the color of our skin, it is safe to assume that our spiritual diet affects the color of our spirit. If we fill our hearts and minds with the things of this world, the color of our spirit will suffer. If we feast on God's Word and spend time in His presence, our spirit will glow with the vibrant colors of spiritual health.

So how do we glow? The apostle Paul gives us some advice. He simply says, "draw near." *"Let us draw near to God with a sincere heart and with the full assurance that faith brings."* (Hebrews 10:22).

What color are you spiritually? We all have areas that have lost their luster. What color do we want to be? Do we want all God has for us or are we tempted to settle for a faded relationship?

God is ready and willing to add vibrant color to our relationship with Him if only we will draw near.

PONDERINGS

~ What color are you spiritually? How would you describe your level of intimacy with God?

~ How does spending time with someone show your love for them? What keeps you from spending more time with God?

~ Read Ephesians 3:14-21. What does this passage teach us about drawing near to God?

O Christ, our Morning Star, Splendor of Light Eternal, shining with the glory of the rainbow, come and waken us from the greyness of our apathy, and renew in us your gift of hope. Amen.
~ Bede the Venerable (672-735)

CAUGHT OFF GUARD

When our daughter, Rhonda, was attending Northern Illinois University, I went to the college one night to join her and her college friends for dinner and a movie. (Allow me to give you some advice. Never let college students pick the movie!) We went to see "Death Trap" with Michael Caine and Christopher Reeve. Partway through the movie, everyone breathed a sigh of relief when the evil man was killed and buried in the backyard. A short time later, however, he came crashing abruptly through a window, alive and well and as evil as ever. Rhonda and her friends were greatly amused at my reaction to the window crashing scene because I nearly jumped out of my chair. I was relaxed and totally unprepared for the sudden turn of events. I was "caught off guard."

Life is like that sometimes. Everything is going well, and we assume everything will continue to go well. When life delivers a sudden blow, our reactions are usually less than constructive. In the Bible, when Moses returned from speaking with God on the mountain, he carried in his hands the 10 Commandments written by the finger of God. When he saw the people worshiping the golden calf, he was suddenly angered and smashed the stone tablets on the ground. He was "caught off guard."

Eve was caught off guard when she listened to the lies of Satan.

Adam was caught off guard when Eve offered him a taste of innocent looking fruit. Lot's wife was caught off guard because she didn't believe God meant what He said. Samson was said to have superhuman strength, yet he was caught off guard by one deceptive female named Delilah. King David was caught off guard by the beauty of Bathsheba.

If the Bible characters were caught off guard so easily, rest assured that we are not immune. But we can learn from their mistakes. *"These things happened to them as examples and were written down as warnings for us... So, if you think you are standing firm, be careful that you don't fall!"* (1 Corinthians 10:11-12) If we are not careful, our life explosions may cause us to say and do things we will regret later.

Just like the man in the movie, evil is NEVER buried and gone. It has a way of resurrecting and crashing into our lives when we least expect it. How do we prepare? *"Watch and pray so that you will not fall into temptation. The spirit is willing, but the flesh is weak."* (Matthew 26:41) Then we will not be "caught off guard!"

PONDERINGS

~ When was the last time something caught you off guard? What was your reaction?

~ When the Bible tells us to "watch and pray," what does it mean to watch?

~ Read 1 Peter 3:15. Have you ever been "caught off guard" in your Christian witness? How do we prepare?

Lord, help us to be prepared so we will not be caught off guard. Sometimes we become so absorbed and exhausted taking care of our day-by-day obligations. Lord, we can't afford to squander our time in frivolity and indulgence. Help us not to loiter or linger. May we be fully prepared for Your will in our lives. Amen.
~ Based on Romans 13:11-14 (MSG)

Watercolor Painting by Janet Bixler

DANGER! DANGER!

My husband's job took him on many overseas business trips. On one of Jack's trips to Tanzania, Africa, their group scheduled a guided safari to the Serengeti, a national park of rolling plains covering 5,700 square miles. It is estimated that some three million large animals call the Serengeti home. He shares the following story.

> During our guided safari, we had to come to a complete stop to wait for an elephant to get off the road. At another spot along the road, we had to slow down as a giraffe was sauntering down the road in front of us. The guide was determined to find some lions for us, but to no avail. On the way to the supposed lion habitat, we stopped at another small lagoon where some hippos were bathing. When hippos bathe, about all one can see above the water are two ears, two eyes and two nostrils. The hippos were on the other side of the lagoon, so I decided to walk around to the other side to get some close-up pictures. I was standing about three feet from the edge of the water with tall grass between me and the water's edge.

I was busily taking my photos when our guide came running down the path toward me shouting, *"Danger, Danger, Crocodile! Danger! Crocodile!"* He grabbed me by the arm and quickly pulled me away. At the same time, we heard a splash and saw Mr. Crocodile slip into the water. From a distance, our guide and the rest of the group had seen him resting in the tall grass at my feet, but I was completely unaware of his presence.

My husband's trip to Tanzania was during the time that the movie, "Crocodile Dundee" was popular in the theaters. So our children made a large sign for the front yard to welcome him home that read, "Welcome home, Crocodile Dad-dee!"

Jack had a close call...one that might have been avoided if he had been more aware of a potential enemy. In the Bible, Satan is depicted as a serpent, a lion or a dragon. It wouldn't surprise me if God had used a Crocodile to describe him. Crocodiles are ruthless, aggressive and count on the element of surprise. That sounds like Satan to me. That's why we are told in 1 Corinthians 16:13 to, *"Be on guard... Be courageous... Be strong."* Jesus calls out to us, *"Danger! Danger!"* and tries to pull us away. Our job is to open our ears, listen, and then yield to His direction.

PONDERINGS

~ Read Psalm 121. What does this Psalm tell us about God's protection?

~ What temps us most to ignore danger warnings? Do we doubt their validity? Do we think we are exempt?

~ Read Isaiah 41:10. What's the difference between being aware of the presence of evil and worrying about it?

> Lord, may it please You to defend us from all dangerous enemies; and in Your mercy and pity to keep us safe in every time of danger and difficulty. Give us a firm hope in Your goodness to us. Amen.
> ~ Sir Gilbert Scott (1811-1878)

RECETA

PARA

EL DESASTRE

RECIPE FOR DISASTER

A missionary from Mexico was visiting our church in Newberry, Michigan. My husband and I, who were youth directors at the time, thought it would be a great idea to invite her to our home for dinner, along with the entire youth group, for an authentic Mexican meal. When having company, it's usually best to stay with tried and true recipes that have worked well in the past, but since I wanted a "real" Mexican meal, I went to the Library and copied some recipes out of a Mexican cookbook. My husband warned me that I should cut down on the hot sauce because most of our guests were not accustomed to eating spicy foods but, since I wanted it to be "authentic," I ignored his request.

You guessed it! The entire youth group missed school the next day with intestinal problems. My husband and I were sick as well. We never found out if the missionary was sick. We were afraid to ask.

Another time when I was having friends over for dinner, I decided to make a pork stir-fry, something I was confident I could do well. The problem surfaced because the bottle of soy sauce and the bottle of Mexican vanilla are almost identical in appearance. Yes, you are right again. I grabbed the Mexican vanilla for my stir fry instead of the soy sauce. In addition to being almost inedible, it was rather embarrassing.

You may enjoy a good chuckle at my expense, but we may as well admit that all of us have probably used a "recipe for disaster" at one time or another. Sometimes we are so anxious to impress or are overconfident in our abilities that we forget what is important. If we are so determined to give company our best, we should, all the more, desire to give God our best! In the Old Testament, God demanded that the sacrifices brought to Him be without defect. *"'When you bring injured, crippled or diseased animals and offer them as sacrifices, should I accept them from your hands?' says the LORD."* (Malachi 1:13)

God does not want our second best, and He does not want our leftovers. The best gift we can give God is the gift of ourselves. *"Do your best to present yourself to God as one approved, a workman who does not need to be ashamed and who correctly handles the word of truth."* (2 Timothy 2:15) Howard B. Grose, (1851-1939) says it best in the following hymn:

> Give of your best to the Master;
> Give Him first place in your heart;
> Give Him first place in your service;
> Consecrate every part.

In His Holy Word, God lays out His recipe for a sanctified life that will please Him. When we carelessly alter life's recipe to suit ourselves, it is always a "recipe for disaster!"

PONDERINGS

~ What's your favorite recipe?

~ Which of our actions show that we are more anxious to please people or ourselves than we are to please God?

~ In which areas of your life do you tend to give God the leftovers, rather than your best? If everyone served God the way you do, what would the world look like?

Lord, sanctify us. Oh! That Your spirit might come and saturate every faculty, subdue every passion, and use every power of our nature for obedience to God. Amen.

~ Charles Spurgeon (1834-1892)

Grandsons Ben and Brad Edwards

IT'S ALL ABOUT BALANCE

Our grandsons, Ben and Brad, ride unicycles. In 2002, after having the unicycles for less than two years, they won some awards at the International Unicycle World Championship competition in Seattle. In 2003, both boys won awards in the National Unicycling Championships in Minneapolis. Ben was the intermediate class-A artistic freestyle national champion and Brad was the overall racing national champion of the 9-10 year-old age group. Our son, Bruce, also rides a unicycle. He shares his own claim to fame in Minneapolis: *"I competed in the one-mile, off-road unicycle course. I did not get last place because I beat two six-year-old girls who got lost in the woods."*

Bruce started a unicycle club in his neighborhood. He called it The Unicycle Uni-Versity. About fifty kids and adults participated, and Bruce owned twenty-six unicycles which he rented to members. There is something intriguing about unicycles - riding is all about balance. Unicyclists have to balance their whole body or they will fall.

Balance is important in OUR lives as well. We must balance work and rest, spending and saving, and even our hearts need a balance of giving love and receiving love. The Christian's lifestyle is also about balance - balancing the desires of the flesh with the desires of the spirit. If we are not careful, it will be lop-sided and we will be off-balance. If our spiritual life is out of balance, we could end up with spiritually skinned knees, or worse yet, with a spiritual concussion.

How do you define a healthy, balanced Christian? Most of the time, God is not asking that we spend time on our knees in a closet 24/7. But He is also not pleased if we go several days without even talking with Him. Luke 2:52 gives a great example of balance. It says that Jesus grew in wisdom, in stature and in favor with God and men. In other words, he grew emotionally, physically, spiritually and socially. Maintaining health in all four of those areas is the only way to be spiritually fit and able to serve God to the best of our abilities.

The best balance of them all is the promise in scripture that tells us to, *"Draw near to God and He will draw near to you...."* (James 4:8 NKJV) That will keep us in perfect balance!

PONDERINGS

~ Which areas of your life seem to be out of balance?

~ How do we find a balance between trusting God and taking action?

~ Read Hebrews 12:1-2. Jesus balanced the joy set before him against the cross. When do WE have similar choices?

Eternal God, in whom we live and move and have our being, cleanse us from all our offenses, and deliver us from proud thoughts and vain desires, that with reverent and humble hearts we may draw near to you, confessing our faults, confiding in your grace, and finding in you our refuge and strength; through Jesus Christ your Son. Amen.   ~ Book of Common Worship (1993)

ADDICTED TO MEDIOCRITY

My sister-in-law, Ginger, was cooking pizza for us during our visit to her home in Payson, Arizona. Although she set the oven to the required temperature and for the required amount of time, the pizzas were doughy and undercooked when she took them out of the oven. Maybe her oven had a variance, or maybe it was because she was cooking two pizzas at once. I have also read that at altitudes over 3000 feet, baked goods may need adjustments in time or temperature and we were at 5000 feet. Whatever the reason, she made the wise decision to put them back into the oven a little longer. When she took the pizzas out the second time, they were perfect.

There is a scripture in Hosea 7:8 that says, "...*Ephraim* (one of the tribes of Israel) *is a flat cake not turned over*." I'm not sure exactly what God is trying to say in this scripture, but I imagine it means that the people of Ephraim were a little "half-baked" like our pizzas. Perhaps they did not spend enough time in the warmth of God's love to allow the finishing touches of His grace to complete their spiritual growth.

Some of us may qualify as half-baked Christians. We have just enough religion to make us miserable. I saw a book one time entitled, "Addicted to Mediocrity." Although I have not read it, I thought the title was intriguing. Are we, as Christians, addicted to mediocrity? Are we content with less than God's best? Do we stray from God's plans for our lives because it seems like too much effort?

There's an idiom that says, *"The good is the enemy of the best."* It's easy to fall into thinking that if it is good enough, the best is unnecessary. How many areas of our lives do we settle for less than excellence? Not one of us would like to be known as a mediocre person, but yet we succumb to laziness. What traits help us to succeed? It definitely takes perseverance. (My mother used to call it "stick-to-itiveness") But it also requires faith and a vision of what could be accomplished if we keep going even when everyone else is lulled into complacency.

If we are half-baked in any area, there are only two things that will finish the baking...time and temperature. Spending time in God's presence in the warmth of His love will eliminate the mediocre. Hebrews 12:12-13 in the Message Bible tells us: *"Don't sit around on your hands! No more dragging your feet! Clear the path for long-distance runners so no one will trip and fall, so no one will step in a hole and sprain an ankle. Help each other out. And run for it!"* There's nothing "mediocre" about that!

PONDERINGS

~ Whom do you admire most for their "stick-to-itiveness"?

~ Would you describe your prayer life as mediocre, on-fire, or somewhere in between? Why?

~ In what areas do you have a tendency to be half-baked? Service to others? Christian witness? Financial giving? Other?

O most loving Father of Jesus Christ, from whom flows all love, let our hearts, frozen in sin, cold to you and cold to others, be warmed by Your divine fire. Amen.
~ Prayer of Anselm (12th Century)

THE GIFT OF FREEDOM

I had a great deal of freedom when I was eleven. In fact, I had entirely too much freedom! My mother could not afford a babysitter during the summer, so the neighbors were supposed to keep a watchful eye on me. Although it was a safer world in 1951, my friends and I never lacked imagination for exciting but risky adventures. We loved playing on the railroad tracks or climbing over the fence at the junk yard to find "good" junk.

One day, my four friends and I were feeling especially brave. We decided to hitchhike from our town of Aurora, Illinois to Naperville, Illinois. We were first picked up by a lonely elderly lady who talked during the whole trip and wished us well on our journey before she dropped us off. We played for a while down by the river. One of my friends fell into the water. We pooled our money to buy her a pair of shorts and hoped her jeans would be dry before she arrived home so that her parents would not find out what had happened.

On the way home, we were picked up by a young man. One friend bravely sat in the front and the rest of us crammed into the back seat. We naively felt very safe because one girl had a jackknife in her pocket. We arrived home safely with no clue of the enormous risk we had just taken. To our chagrin, one of my friends felt guilty and confessed to her parents, getting us all into big trouble.

159

It goes without saying that five innocent young girls should not have been hitchhiking with strangers. I am extremely grateful we did not end up as a tragic statistic. Yes, as a child, I had a lot of freedom, but through the misuse of that freedom, I put myself and others in great danger. As we grow older, it should mean that we handle our freedoms wisely. Unfortunately, that is not always the case.

We all love freedom, but in our quest to be free, we can make choices that put us into bondage. Wisdom is knowing which freedoms make us truly free. Rabindranath Tagore (1861-1941) spoke this truth, *"Emancipation from the bondage of the soil is no freedom for the tree."* Certain restrictions exist for our benefit. May God give us the wisdom to know which rules we need and which ones we should challenge.

As we exercise our freedom to make choices, let us make sure we use wisdom in the most important choice of all. *"...Choose for yourselves this day whom you will serve.... but as for me and for my house, we will serve the Lord."* (Joshua 24:15)

"If the Son sets you free, you will be free indeed. (John 8:36)

PONDERINGS

~ What freedoms do you enjoy? Where do you feel trapped in slavery?

~ Romans 6:14 says we are not under the law and yet, Galatians 5:14 talks about keeping the law. Are these verses in conflict?

~ When is striving for freedom motivated by selfish desires?

Enter my heart, O Holy Spirit, come in blessed mercy and set me free. Throw open, O Lord, the locked doors and my mind; O Holy Spirit, very God, whose presence is liberty, grant me the perfect freedom - to be your servant, today, tomorrow and evermore. Amen.   ~ St Anselm (1033-1109)

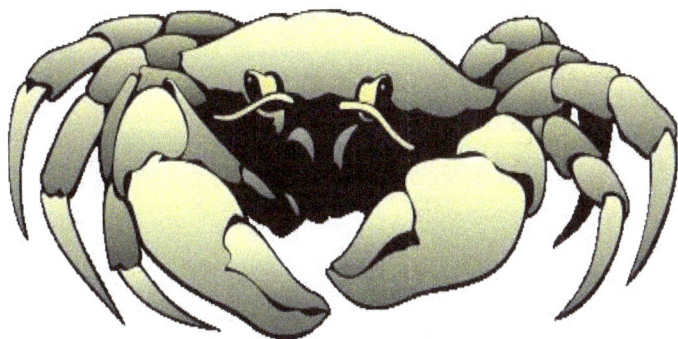

CRABBY

When we lived in Maryland, we loved to go crabbing for Maryland Blue Crabs in the Chesapeake Bay. Our children enjoyed catching crabs the old-fashioned way by dangling a raw chicken neck on a string into the water. When they felt a tug on the string, they would use a long-handled pole with a landing net to scoop up the crab. The trick was getting the crab into the pail. To the inexperienced, it would seem like a simple matter to turn the net upside down over the bucket and dump it out. Crabs, however, tend to be a little crabby and use their claws to tightly clamp onto the net, avoiding the bucket at all costs.

We used long-handled tongs to pry their claws loose. Sometimes this method worked, sometimes it didn't. If we made the mistake of holding the net close to the edge of the bucket, the crab would quickly scramble over the side, scurry sideways across the boardwalk and plunge into the bay to freedom. It was always fun to watch our barefooted children scream and dance, keeping their toes out of harm's way until the crab dropped into the water.

We would try tempting the crabs with a nice bucket of bay water. Some got tired of holding on, relaxed their grip and dropped into our pail. Others were stubborn, and it seemed impossible to pry them loose. Our little crabs had every reason to be crabby - we were trying to take them captive. We were not only taking away their freedom, but also threatening their lives.

We are in danger of being taken captive as well... by Satan. He wants us to release our grip on our values and beliefs. The Bible tells us: *"Be self-controlled and alert. Your enemy, the devil, prowls around like a roaring lion looking for someone to devour."* (1 Peter 5:8) The real problem is that he doesn't look like a lion. 2 Corinthians 11:13 tells us that, *"Satan himself masquerades as an angel of light."*

Some of our little crabs were smart enough to know that the enticing bucket of water below them was a trap and not at all equal to swimming free in the Bay. It pays to be a little crabby when it comes to temptation. We must not take the dangers lightly. Sometimes we tire of holding on, relax our grip and succumb to the plans of the enemy.

The Bible tells us: *"...Resist the devil, and he will flee from you."* (James 4:7) Jesus was just a little crabby in his response to the temptations of Satan. He quoted scripture and simply said, *"...Beat it, Satan!..."* (Matthew 4:10 - MSG) It's time for us to get "crabby" with the devil!

PONDERINGS

~ How alluring is a fresh bucket of instant gratification? What tempts you most to release your grip on God's priorities?

~ What is the best way to inform Satan that our resolve cannot and will not be broken?

~ Read Ephesians 6:10-17. What advice do you see for strengthening your grip and getting crabby with the devil?

Loving Father, we ask you accept our good commitments, ones that You inspired through the Holy Spirit. Strengthen our resolve, we ask, by your grace. Let no sudden desires, powerful inclinations, poor purposes and half-way actions lead us astray. Instead, may we demonstrate the fruits of righteous living, given by Jesus. Amen. ~ John Wesley (1703-1791)

LAUGHTER, THE BEST MEDICINE

There is nothing more refreshing than the sound of laughter. I love it when my grandchildren get the giggles. The sound makes the whole house come alive. We had an experience one time at Michigamme United Methodist Family Camp that gave our family a good laugh.

On Thursday evening at camp, the log chapel was set up for communion. After a brief service in the dining hall, each family was invited to go to the chapel privately to take communion. When our turn came, we entered the chapel and seated ourselves around the communion table on wooden folding chairs. As my husband, Jack, sat down, we heard a loud crack as the chair collapsed. He quietly and reverently set the broken chair aside, replacing it with another one, but as soon as he sat down, the second chair broke as well. This time, not so reverently and amid snickers from the family, he again replaced the chair. When the third chair broke, the atmosphere was anything but reverent. The family doubled over with laughter. Although the fourth chair held, we were sure we heard God laughing as well. The humor continued into the following year when someone called out as we arrived, *"Hide the chairs, Jack's here!"*

We need laughter! Many times, our lives are filled with stress, which, in turn, drains our energy and dampens our enthusiasm. Jesus wants us to have joy. *"I have told you this so that my joy may be in you and that your joy may be complete."* (John 15:11)

If we find that joy is lacking in our lives, where do we look for it? Johann Wolfgang von Goethe (1749-1832) said, *"Who is the happiest of men? He who values the merits of others, and in their pleasure takes joy, even as though it were his own."* Perhaps if we try making others happy, we will not have to search for joy - it will find us. And when it does, we will enjoy the benefits.

A joyful spirit is good for us! It triggers the release of endorphins, which are natural feel-good chemicals, giving us a sense of well-being. Proverbs 17:22 tells us that, *"A cheerful heart is good medicine, but a crushed spirit dries up the bones."*

Henry Ward Beecher (1813-1887) said, *"Mirth is God's medicine. Everybody ought to bathe in it."* Yes, laughter is the best medicine! The gift of laughter is truly one of God's greatest gifts.

PONDERINGS

~ What makes you laugh? Is laughter contagious? Is joy a choice? Why or why not?

~ Have you ever thought of laughter as medicinal? How important are joyful memories?

~ Read Psalm 126:1-3. On a scale of 1 to 10, where would you rate their joy? How would you rate YOUR joy?

LORD, you are my Lord; apart from you I have no good thing. You have made known to me the path of life; you will fill me with joy in your presence, with eternal pleasures at your right hand. Amen.
~ Psalm 16:1,11

Pepcon Explosion, Henderson, NV, May 4, 1988

DECONTAMINATION

Shortly after we moved to Las Vegas, Nevada in 1988, there was a major explosion at Pepcon, an ammonium perchlorate processing plant in Henderson, south of Las Vegas. Both my husband and I heard the noise and rushed outside to see the plume of smoke rising in the air. Although the plant was five miles from our house, our front door and an upstairs window were damaged.

The Pepcon disaster claimed two lives and injured 372 people. Ammonium perchlorate is used as an oxidizer in space vehicles and is highly volatile. The explosion was massive because there was an estimated 4000 tons of the product stored at the site and there was a high-pressure natural gas line running underneath the plant which ruptured during one of the explosions. A total of seven explosions caused close to $100 million in damages. The largest explosion measured 3.5 on the Richter scale. Since my husband worked for the Office of Pipeline Safety for the State of Nevada, he was called to investigate the accident. He says:

> The explosion created a cavern and ripped up a 16-inch natural gas line going through the property. I spent most of my first summer out in the desert at the site. I've never drunk so much Gatorade in my life. Adjacent to this facility was a Kidd

165

Marshmallow factory that was also completely leveled. Do you know, marshmallows do not come out the best during an explosion? What a sticky gooey mess all over the place!

When entering contaminated areas, we had to wear the traditional white "monkey suits," designed so air will not penetrate them. Afterwards, we would stand in a kid's inflatable wading pool to be hosed down. Then we would remove our boots and pour about a quart of perspiration out of each boot. This was tough work for a north-woodsman like me who cannot take hot weather.

As Christians, we are continually in danger of contamination from our sinful world. Toxic attitudes and cultural influences can put our souls in danger. It's important that we cleanse ourselves of these worldly impurities by spending time in the presence of God, allowing His healing love to wash over us. Let the "decontamination" process begin!

"Since we have these promises, dear friends, let us purify ourselves from everything that contaminates body and spirit, perfecting holiness out of reverence for God." (2 Corinthians 7:1)

PONDERINGS

~ Read 2 Corinthians 6:17. How do we decide which values of the world are unclean?

~ Should we limit contact with the world? How then do we find opportunities for witnessing?

~ Read Romans 12:2. What does it mean to not "conform" to the pattern of this world?"

Thank you, Jesus, that your blood purifies me from all sin. You have promised that if I confess my sin, you are faithful and just and will forgive my sin and purify me from all unrighteousness. Amen.   ~ Based on 1 John 1:7,9

Photo by Janet Hatfield

A ROSE BY ANY OTHER NAME

The title above comes from a quote in Shakespeare's play, Romeo and Juliet... *"A rose by any other name would smell as sweet."* As a young child, I hated my name. I was named after my grandmother, Idella Pearl Chapin. Kids love to make fun of unique names, so my maiden name, Idella Liskey, gave my classmates ample ammunition to make fun of me. I was a shy kid, and the barbs stung. They would taunt me on a regular basis with chants such as, *"Idella Liskey loves whiskey,"* or *"Ideller has a feller in the cellar."* Kids can be cruel.

As I matured, I began to love my name. I have met only a small number of people in my lifetime with the same first name as mine. One time, by coincidence, I happened to sit next to a lady on an airplane whose name was Idella.

Names are important. We always knew we were in trouble when our mother called us by our full names. Husbands and wives usually have pet names for each other such as "honey," "sweetheart" or even "my little turtle dove." Sometimes we have pet nicknames for our children. My father used to call me "Bedo" but I never knew where the name came from. My daughter called our grandson Samuel "Bambino," the Italian name for "little boy." Later it became "Sambeeno" and eventually ended up as "Beeno."

Yes, names are important, but if we change the name, it does not change the person.... "a rose by any other name...." Parents take great care when choosing names for their children. Sometimes they name them after their favorite relatives or even Bible characters. (Of course, there are plenty of names in the Bible that DON'T seem as popular, such as Abishag, Elishama, Jaazaniah or Habazziniah.) lol

One of the methods parents use to encourage proper behavior in their children is reminding them that, no matter where they are or what they are doing, they should always *"remember who they are"* and bring honor to the family name. Socrates once wrote: *"Regard your name as the richest jewel you can possibly possess."*

The word "Christian" includes the name of "Christ." When we claim the title of "Christian" as our own, it is imperative that we "remember who we are." Everything we do should bring honor to that name.

Colossians 3:17 tells us, *"Whatever you do, whether in word or deed, do it all in the NAME of the LORD JESUS, giving thanks to God the Father through him."*

PONDERINGS

~ How do most people decide what to name their child? After a relative or someone famous?

~ List as many names for Jesus (given in the Bible) that you can think of. What do they tell you about Him?

~ Read Proverbs 22:1. Do you agree? Why is so much emphasis put on a name?

O Heavenly Father, breathe into our souls the love of whatsoever is true and beautiful and good. May we fear to be unfaithful, and have no other fear. Help us to remember that we are your children, and belong to you. Amen. ~ William Angus Knight (1836–1916)

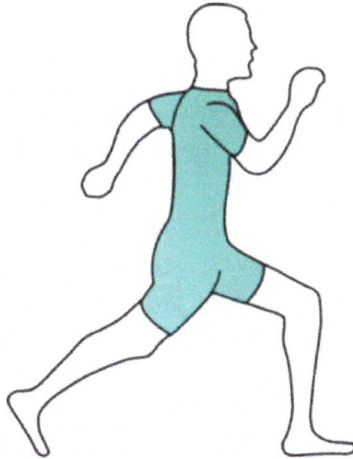

CHOOSE LIFE

Life is full of decisions. When our grandson, Ben Edwards, was 21, he shared a true-life illustration of the decision making process:

Today, I woke up, and I didn't want to go running. I wanted to lie in bed because my bed was so comfortable, and it was raining outside. I felt like I wouldn't have fun running, my muscles would just hurt and I'd be cold and wet. It would be miserable and not worth it. I could just wake up and make some hot chai tea and sit with a blanket in my bed. It would be so much easier, and I wouldn't have to go through all the effort. But I got myself up, put in my contacts, got dressed and went out into the cold.

I didn't want to be there at the start, but as I began to run, I warmed up. My cold legs didn't cramp and were comfortable. It was peaceful, relaxing even - being alone and just hearing the rain. It was nothing like I expected or felt it would be. When I got back I was drenched, but my once cold apartment that I woke up in felt warm and cozy.

After a hot shower, I weighed myself and found I had lost a pound. Since I've been running in the mornings, I feel more awake. It's also helped me with staying awake in classes and just feeling more productive. I'm glad I went running even though I didn't want to!

To Ben, it would have felt better to curl up under a blanket, but because he made the choice to run, he felt more alive. The Bible verse below tells us that if we want God's blessings, we must "choose life." *"This day I call heaven and earth as witnesses against you that I have set before you life and death, blessings and curses. Now choose life, so that you and your children may live and that you may love the LORD your God, listen to his voice and hold fast to him..."* (Deuteronomy 30:19-20a)

Life is full of choices - too many to count. Some choices are trivial, others drastically change our lives. We choose everything from the food we eat to the attitudes we adopt. Some choices are made out of habit, while others require deliberation.

Making right choices has a snowball effect. When we do the right thing, we are happy with ourselves. Just as Ben said, *"I'm glad I went running even though I didn't want to."* Those positive emotions make it easier to make right choices the next time. When we "choose life," God never runs out of blessings!

PONDERINGS

~ What difficult decisions have you had to make?

~ In what ways do music, media or friends affect the choices we make? Is this good or bad?

~ Read Esther 4:15-16. How difficult was Esther's decision? What was at stake? How does dwelling on the outcome of our decisions affect our choices?

O God, Grant us, in all our doubts and uncertainties, the grace to ask what you would have us to do, that the Spirit of wisdom may save us from all false choices, and that in your light we may see light, and in your straight path may not stumble; through Jesus Christ our Lord. Amen.   ~ Book of Common Prayer (1549)

Quilt by Sharon Johnson

ITCHING TO BE STITCHING

My friend, Becki Flood, came for a visit from Oklahoma to our home in Marion, IL. We wanted her to have a good time and since she is a quilter, my husband and I took Becki and her daughter, Lesly, to tour the National Quilt Museum in Paducah, Kentucky. The museum attracts about 40,000 visitors annually and contains over 150 antique and contemporary quilts. I have never done any quilting, so I was thoroughly prepared for a long, boring afternoon. I found myself, however, blown away by the intricate craftsmanship, amazing creativity and sheer beauty of the quilts on display.

One thing common to all quilters - they are always "itching to be stitching." They love what they do. Quilters get a bigger thrill out of shopping for material than for new clothes. They have even been known to visit fabric stores while on vacation.

A master quilter can create a thing of beauty from an ordinary pile of scraps. To a quilter, a bed without a quilt is like a sky without stars. One of the crucial aspects of quilting is choosing the right fabric: the right texture, the right colors, the right patterns and even the right personality to fit the uniqueness of the person who will receive it.

171

To ensure the quilt will be cherished for years to come and then passed on to future generations, the craftsmanship must be superior. A serious quilter must have the gifts of patience, perseverance and tenacity. My talented friend, Sharon Johnson, has those gifts. One of my favorite quilts that she made has several types of birds on it. Because I have a new appreciation for quilts and because I am a bird lover, it combines the best of both worlds.

Our lives are like quilts. Sometimes life hands us only a pile of scraps, but it's up to us to use our God-given talents and creativity to make a masterpiece. Quilts often tell stories by reflecting memories or historical events. Our lives tell stories as well. What we value most in life is clearly demonstrated by our daily attitudes and actions.

Each piece of our life's quilt should reflect the fruit of the Spirit from Galatians 5:22-23: *"...the fruit of the Spirit is love, joy, peace, patience, kindness, goodness, faithfulness, gentleness and self-control..."* Because we have the support of the Holy Spirit, we should be "itching to be stitching" a life that is pleasing to our Heavenly Father and one that will inspire others for generations to come.

PONDERINGS

~ What talents has God given you? When do you feel the most creative?

~ Read Romans 8:28. How does that apply to the "pile of scraps" in your life?

~ What would help you visualize the masterpiece God has in mind for you? How does visualization help?

Lord, I pray that, being rooted and established in love, I may have power, together with all the saints, to grasp how wide and long and high and deep is your love so that I may be filled to the measure of all your fullness. Amen.   ~ based on Ephesians 3:17-19

172

Photo by Bruce Edwards

GOING BATTY

My husband went into the garage at our home in southern Illinois and picked up what he thought was a dried-up leaf on the floor. When it started to wiggle, he realized he was holding the wing of a small bat. He placed it on top of a bush outside and hoped it would survive.

Another "batty" experience occurred when we lived in Tornado, West Virginia. We heard scratching noises from inside the downspout on the side of our garage. Thinking a bird was stuck inside the pipe, my husband put the water hose in the top and turned the water on. What flushed out the bottom of the pipe was a very angry bat with its teeth bared! My husband covered the bat with a broom and swept it down the hill while I quickly went inside the house.

There are approximately 1000 species of bats in the world. They have been around since the age of the dinosaur. Most people do not like bats, but bats are very beneficial. They help get rid of mosquitoes and keep gardens free of insects. One little bat can catch over 600 mosquitoes in an hour. A bat can consume almost 50% of its body weight in insects (moths, mosquitoes, flies and beetles) in one night. Another intriguing characteristic of bats is their unique sonar system. They are capable of emitting high-pitched squeals, up to 200 pulses per second. When the sound hits an object, an echo bounces back to the bat's ears revealing details about the distance, size and shape of the object, enabling bats to fly safely in total darkness.

Sometimes life drives us "batty." In an instant, our world can turn dark and dismal, making us feel like we are inside a pipe, scratching frantically to be free.

Our greatest need in the midst of high stress is a spiritual one. A close relationship with the Almighty God of the Universe will soothe our fears even when our inner turmoil leaves every nerve ending raw. God is the great Comforter! *"Come to me, all you who are weary and burdened, and I will give you rest. Take my yoke upon you and learn from me, for I am gentle and humble in heart, and you will find rest for your souls."* (Matthew 11:28-29)

If we stay grounded in God's Word, using the sonar system of the Holy Spirit to help us navigate through life's dark and frightening pathways, we will never go "batty" because *"...the Spirit helps us in our weakness..."* (Romans 8:26)

PONDERINGS

~ What's been driving you batty lately? How do you usually deal with stress?

~ Read Matthew 6:25-34. How does this scripture help you cope with stress?

~ Read John 14:27. How was it possible for Jesus to have peace, knowing what the future held for Him?

O God and Father of us all, breathe upon us now your hallowed calm; lift the burden from our hearts, soothe the anxieties of our minds and send peace into our souls. Help us now to stand while in the shelter of your shadowing wings, and to be still, to wait for the revelation of your will that shall make us calm and strong. Amen.
~ W. E. Orchard (1877-1955)

UNCONDITIONAL LOVE

My daughter Rhonda, who is a nurse, told me about her new patient. She said: *"I'm dialyzing a prisoner tomorrow. Liver failure, hepatitis, kidney failure - comes with a guard."*

Sometimes, our society is less than sympathetic to people when their problems are the direct results of their bad choices. I wondered how my daughter felt about doing dialysis on a prisoner, so I asked her if she was uncomfortable. Her response...

No, it doesn't make me uncomfortable, and I kind of have a heart for them. This guy today was in a lot of pain but can't have narcotics for pain. He was also quite incoherent from end stage liver failure induced encephalopathy. His brain is failing. He's only 43 and is bright yellow from jaundice. He was a DNR (do not resuscitate) but it was reversed until they could find family members to support the decision. They haven't found any.

I have always been impressed with the depth of Rhonda's compassion. Her experience raised questions in my own mind. If I had been exposed to the same circumstances during my life as this prisoner, would I have made the same choices? They could not find any family members. How does it feel to have no family or at least none that care? What experiences shaped his sense of self-worth as a child? Did he feel loved?

But compassion is more than pity. Rhonda not only had a heart for her prisoner, she also used her skills in an attempt to alleviate his suffering, and she treated him with kindness. The dictionary says compassion is: *"A feeling of deep sympathy and sorrow for another who is stricken by misfortune, accompanied by a strong desire to alleviate the suffering."* In other words, true compassion leads to action.

If we, as humans, can manage to show compassion to each other, imagine how much more our compassionate God is willing to help us! I love the image in Hosea 11:4. *"I led them with cords of human kindness, with ties of love; I lifted the yoke from their neck and bent down to feed them."* Our Holy God is so full of love for His children that that he bends down to fulfill their needs!

Many times our physical, emotional and spiritual problems are the direct result of our own bad choices. We feel guilty and anticipate His condemnation and anger, but Psalm 116:5 tells us: *"The Lord is gracious and righteous; our God is full of compassion."*

We don't have to earn God's love. We don't have to be perfect to deserve His love. God's love is unconditional!

PONDERINGS

~ Who is one of the most compassionate people you know, and why do you think so?

~ How much compassion do I have for those who do not live up to my standards?

~ If I fully understood the depths of God's love, how would it increase my desire to please Him?

O Lord, give us grace to be just and upright in all our dealings; quiet and peaceable; full of compassion; and ready to do good to all men, according to our abilities and opportunities. Direct us in all our ways. Amen.   ~ 1789 Book of Common Prayer

Ramps

ODORIFEROUS

What's that smell? Anytime we detect a bad odor, we do not hesitate to complain. We don't like bad smells. That's probably why we wear deodorant and stay away from skunks. Yet, there are thousands who gravitate to the stinky Ramp Festival in Richwood, West Virginia. Ramps are wild leeks and supposedly the sweetest tasting and vilest smelling vegetables in nature. School children with ramp odor have been excused from school for several days.

I tasted ramps one time and once was enough! Ramps grow wild, are a staple for the locals and considered to have properties like a spring tonic. Members of the fire department begin digging ramps a week before the festival and fill 20 - 30 trash bags with them.

One of the highlights of the festival is a recipe contest, which includes such delicacies as ramp candy, ramp cornbread, ramp au gratin and creamy ramp risotto. One year the winner won the $500 top prize with his "ramped-up steak sandwich" and also walked off with the "most repugnant" award. He was given a basket full of breath mints and a bottle of Listerine.

There is an abundance of smelly things in this world we try to avoid – like doggy breath and rotten eggs for example. There is, however, an abundance of rich wonderful smells. I love the smell

177

of the air after a spring thunderstorm, the sweet smell of a rose or the tantalizing odor of freshly-baked bread. My daughter, Rhonda, told me one day that she had baked bread with my granddaughter:

Christine and I made whole-wheat bread today in the bread machine. The bread's been in the machine for almost five hours and is almost done. It smells pretty good, and Christine keeps coming in to look at it. She said, *"I just can't get that bread off my mind!"*

God considers us to be the sweet fragrance of Christ. *"For we are to God the aroma of Christ among those who are being saved and those who are perishing."* (2 Corinthians 2:15) There is no higher compliment than that. IF we are to be the "aroma of Christ," we must be more like Him in everything. Our goal is to be like Jesus in our daily choices, our character and our love for others.

Probably most of us have never heard of ramps, nor is visiting a Ramp Festival high on our list of priorities. When it comes to good smells, however, it should be a high priority for us to be the "aroma of Christ" to the world! Hopefully, once they get to know us, they will say, *"I just can't get Jesus off my mind!"*

PONDERINGS

~ What's your favorite smell? How does smell stimulate the appetite? How important does that make the aroma of Christ?

~ In what ways can you be the sweet fragrance of Christ to your family? You friends? Your neighbors?

~ In what ways can other Christians be the aroma of Christ for you?

O Lord my God, may I put off my old self, which is being corrupted by its deceitful desires, to be made new in the attitude of my mind and to put on the new self, created to be like you in true righteousness and holiness. Amen. ~ Based on Ephesians 4:22-24

Idella Pearl Photos

THE STORMS OF LIFE

Have you ever noticed how the storms of life encourage us to reevaluate our priorities? In 2009, our town of Marion, Illinois had a derecho or an inland hurricane. The 88 m.p.h. straight-line winds whipped through five counties with wind gusts up to 106 m.p.h. The Governor declared all five counties disaster areas. Although our house escaped damage, we watched as the wind ripped tiles off our neighbor's roof and sailed them through the air like a deck of cards. Large, beautiful oak trees were uprooted as if they were spindly saplings. We lost our electricity for 47 hours, and some areas were out as long as two weeks.

When we lost electricity, I first worried about how I would finish my computer project. Then I fretted that we would not be able to take hot showers. As time went on, we thought about the food that would spoil in our freezer. Neither telephones nor cell phones were working, so we were unable to monitor the safety of family and friends. My daughter and family live a half mile from us. What we thought was a simple solution (drive over to their house to check on them) turned out to be an impossible task because the side roads were blocked with large fallen trees.

Then we began to wonder about the hospitals and if the nurses could get to work. Were the neighborhood shut-ins safe in the dark? Would there be any house fires set by the careless use of candles? Was anyone hurt in the storm? Our initial reactions were focused on the comforts of life we were missing, but after a while, our reactions were focused on the needs of others. Compassion blossomed throughout town as volunteers pooled their talents, donating hours of labor to assist where needed. Members of the Southern Baptist Convention Disaster Relief Chainsaw Gang worked tirelessly, cutting trees that blocked the roads and homes.

When the "storms of life" subside - the winds die down, the electricity comes back on and we get a hot cup of coffee and a hot shower - do we revert back to our old self-focused ways of thinking? How important are the thoughts and priorities that swirl in our heads in comparison with God's holy plans and purposes? How many of our daily activities are so securely wrapped in our own desires that they exclude everyone else, including God?

Maybe one purpose for the "storms of life" is simply to remind us that life is not all about us. The Bible tells us: *"Let no one seek his own, but each one the other's well-being."* (1 Corinthians 10:24)

PONDERINGS

~ What is the biggest storm in your life right now? What are you doing to cope?

~ Read Mark 4:35-41. How was Jesus able to sleep during a wild storm like that?

~ How good are you at setting priorities? In what ways do the storms of life change priorities?

Be, O God, a Refuge from the storm, and a Shadow from the heat. Lo, help our unbelief, and, in your tenderness, assure us of your protection. You can make all things work together for good to them that love you. Let not calamity injure our souls; let not sorrow corrode our hearts. Amen.   ~ John Hunter (1892)

Brad Edwards

FAMOUS LAST KICK

Our grandson, Brad, has always done well in sports, specifically soccer and track. In his freshman year of high school, he competed in the 1600m race. His father (our son, Bruce) relays the following information about a particular event:

> In the 1600m run, Brad was really seeking to break the five minute mark for the first time. He came close again last night with another personal best of five minutes, 6.3 seconds. There was a field of about 15 runners. Right from the start, Brad jumped out to the lead, but halfway through the second lap, he let two runners go ahead, but kept them at his front door. In the fourth and final lap, one of the leaders tuckered out and Brad blew by him. Then at the 150m mark, Brad pulled out his "famous last kick" and took the front runner with about 10 meters to go before the finish. Everyone was on their feet cheering. It was great!

These are the words of one proud papa. Obviously, Bruce had reason to be proud. When all of Brad's energy was gone, he was still able to reach down deep inside himself and find the hidden resources necessary to excel.

181

The opposite was true of King Jeroboam in Bible times. Jerusalem was a holy city, the center of worship for the Israelites, but instead of having the people journey to Jerusalem, Jeroboam set up substitute places of worship. "...*the king made two golden calves. He said to the people, 'It is too much for you to go up to Jerusalem. Here are your gods, O Israel, who brought you up out of Egypt.' One he set up in Bethel, and the other in Dan.*" (1 Kings 12:28-29)

Is there a Bethel or a Dan in our lives as well? Perhaps it's that place that is easy to get to by following the path of least resistance. We want everything to be easy, including our prayer life. Just give us a formula that works every time - show us the right position, the right words to say and presto, God will reach down His finger of blessing to give us the answer we want.

We are sometimes unwilling to draw on the hidden resources of God's power for that "famous last kick" that propels us to victory. There are many times in life when we think we have gone as far as we can go, but God's power is available! "*Oh, the utter extravagance of his work in us who trust him - endless energy, boundless strength!*" (Ephesians 1:19 - MSG) I think King David said it best in 2 Samuel 22:30: "...*with my God I can scale a wall.*"

PONDERINGS

~ Have you ever been in a race? What kind of a race does a Christian run? What "hidden resources" do we have?

~ Is your family known for their fortitude? How easily do you give up?

~ Who has impressed you by going above and beyond with a "famous last kick"?

Teach us, good Lord, to serve you as you deserve: to give, and not to count the cost; to fight, and not to heed the wounds; to toil, and not to seek for rest; to labor, and not to ask for any reward, except that of knowing that we do your holy will; through Jesus Christ our Lord. Amen.   ~ Ignatius Loyola (1491-1556)

Dean Church

REMEMBERING THE PAST

We all have memories. Oscar Wilde (1854-1900) said, *"Memory is the diary that we all carry about with us."* The human brain has the capacity to store a mind-boggling amount of information, and memory plays a big role in our lives. We can remember skills we have learned, or retrieve stored information, or recall a precious moment from the past.

My friend, Dean, shared the following memory with me:

My name is Dean Lewis Church. I was born to John and Lula Mcfarland Lewis in 1928 in Eagan, Tennessee, the 7th child of 13. Mama and Daddy were expecting their 8th child when I was 4 years old, and that event is my first memory.

My oldest sister, Mabel, age 18, was married and lived nearby. When Mama started into labor, they sent for her. All of us kids were sent to a neighbor's house. When Dr. Butterworth came, Mama had already given birth to a girl, Baby #1, who died shortly after birth. After Baby #2, a boy, was born, the doctor handed him to Mabel who was waiting in the doorway. Then Baby #3, a boy, and Baby #4, a girl, were handed to Mabel as well. Mabel was crying by then and said, *"Doctor, I can't hold any more babies!"* Two boys and two girls, tiny beyond belief, had been born in a tiny four-room house to a poor family.

183

Mama told us we could name the babies and every night we would call out names, but one night, Mama told us she had the babies named: John, Joe, Jean and Jane. To this day, we always say their names in that order.

The Public Health Nurse brought a homemade baby bed. It had a wooden frame with screen wire tacked around the sides. Bricks, warmed on the hearth and wrapped in towels, surrounded the babies. Diapers were made from folded men's handkerchiefs. The babies were fed with medicine droppers. People came from everywhere to see the babies. A package came from California containing sweaters, caps, and booties, but we never knew how she heard about the story.

Baby #1 had died the first day, Baby #2 died 10 days later and Baby #4 lived only 47 days. Baby #3, John, lived to be 80 years old and died in 2012. I remember the tiny caskets in the front room. Nickels were placed on their eyes. Mama had two more babies, making 13 in all. I am the last child living, and I am 88. I never get tired of telling of my first memory.

Memories are a valuable part of who we are. Christians, of all people, need to have good memories. We must remember to count our blessings, to remember that this world is not our home and, most of all to remember to, *"Love the Lord your God with all your heart and with all your soul and with all your mind."* and to *"Love your neighbor as yourself."* (Matthew 22:37-39)

PONDERINGS

~ What is your favorite memory?

~ What methods do you use to remember important things?

~ What do you want to be remembered for when you are gone? What are you doing now to make that happen?

Lord, I will remember your miracles of long ago. I will consider all your works and meditate on all your mighty deeds. Your ways, God, are holy. Amen. (Psalm 77:11-13)

Mother, Esther

Granddaughter, Meghan

LEAVING A LEGACY

My mother, Esther, passed away in January of 2009 at the age of 100. God instructs us to learn from previous generations: *"This is what the Lord says: 'Stand at the crossroads and look; ask for the ancient paths, ask where the good way is, and walk in it, and you will find rest for your souls...'"* (Jeremiah 6:16) It's easy to learn from my mother's life because she left such a great legacy - not only through her stories, poems and piano music, but also through her generous, unselfish nature. Her life blessed others.

We all leave legacies for future generations. The question is what kind? If we were asked what we would like our headstones to read, I wonder what we would choose.

When our granddaughter, Meghan, was 11 years old, she had a school assignment to write poetry and to make a list of her favorite poems by other poets. She said:

> I had fun writing the poems for my poem book. I enjoyed reading my grandma's and my nana's poems. I learned it was not so hard to write a poem and it was fun to read it when it was

all done. My favorite poems are 'Time Passes On' and 'One Night I Dreamt of Heaven' written by my nana.

When my nana died, my brother and I read these poems at her funeral. They were interesting and talked of God's love and promises for us. I will always remember these two poems because it was an honor to read them at her funeral, and I will always remember my Nana.

What kind of legacy are we leaving? Realizing that our influence, good or bad, will live for years to come may inspire us to take notice of the trail we are leaving. The legacy my mother left was one of a life lived from the heart. She advises us to do the same in the first stanza of her poem, "Time Passes On."

> Time passes on and what does it bring?
> Time brings changes to everything.
> How do you cope? Where do you start?
> The best thing to do is follow your heart!

The heart is made for love - not love of self, but love for God and others. Following our hearts means listening to the still, small voice of God and making the daily choices that leave an inspiring trail for others to follow. That, my friends, is the best legacy of all!

PONDERINGS

~ Is there a particular person who left you a significant legacy (for better or for worse)?

~ What kind of legacy does the world encourage you to leave and how is that different from what God desires?

~ If you could choose one of your traits to pass on to future generations, which one would it be?

Your throne, O God, will last for ever and ever. I will make Your name to be remembered in all generations: therefore shall the people praise You for ever and ever. Amen.

(Based on Psalm 45:6, 17.)

Mary Hensley

DREAM ON

What is your dream? Do you remember what you dreamt when you were young? Maybe, as you gazed into the stars, you could see yourself flying through the sky. As you grew older, your thoughts were filled with finding just the right person to marry. Then you thought about owning a home. It's exciting to explore all the possibilities! Many times, however, our dreams evaporate as quickly as a drop of water on a hot skillet.

My daughter, Kerry's friend, Mary Hensley, shared her dream with me. At the time, she was living in a trailer home with her husband and three small children. Listen to the way she describes her dream. It is so vivid, we have x-ray vision into her very heart and soul:

> My dream is a house of my own; something big and rambling with a huge yard. My bedroom will be filled with windows... drenched every morning with soft shafts of sunlight. My kitchen will be bright and cheerful...smelling of freshly baked bread. My family room will be constantly messy, strewn with toys and filled with signs of life and love. My dining room will not be a showpiece, but rather the center of our life.

I'll have a huge old oak table, lovingly restored to its former glory - the kind of table you wish could talk so it could share the secrets it has heard over the years - stories of jubilance, sorrow, puppy love and dark nights of the soul. The centerpiece would be a huge white, slightly chipped crockery vase filled daily with fresh wildflowers gathered by my baby girl.

In the yard will be an ancient tree. In its branches will be a tree house built by the boys and their dad. Another branch will host a swing and carved in the tree trunk will be a heart and the initials of my daughter's first secret love. And last, but not least, will be my front porch. At one end, a wooden porch swing cradled beneath boughs of wisteria. Private, yet strategically placed, so when sitting in his recliner, Dad can discreetly view it through delicate lacy curtains. Yeah, this is my dream!

What is your dream? Never give up! There are some things that will never materialize without a dream. Dream on, regardless of the heartache of past failures. Dream on, regardless of the giants looming on the horizon. God is the God of the "possible." Jesus said in Luke 18:27, *"What is impossible with men is possible with God."* Dream on!

PONDERINGS

~ What is your dream? Has your dream changed through the years?

~ Read Proverbs 13:12. What happens to us when our hopes are delayed?

~ How much hope do I have for the future? What can I do to have more hope? Is hope contagious?

O God, grant to us to dream great dreams and not to disobey the heavenly vision, and though the hope seem forlorn, may we be found ready to lead it. However black the night, let the morning star shine in the sky. Amen.   ~ W. E. Orchard (1877-1955)

CONCLUSION

There are two kinds of people: those who say to God,
"Thy will be done,"
...and those to whom God says,
"All right, then, have it your way."

~ C.S. Lewis

The fast track to losing hope is to go our own way. God's way, no matter our circumstances, gives us hope for the future. Somewhere in these meditations, I pray there is one "just for you!" If you feel a renewed hope, we will give God the praise.

In the book of Lamentations, the Message Bible talks about the value of memory. We vividly remember all the bad things that happen to us, but remembering God's power and God's love gives us hope. Which one we dwell on is a choice, and that choice makes all the difference.

I'll never forget the trouble, the utter lostness, the taste of ashes, the poison I've swallowed. I remember it all - oh, how well I remember - the feeling of hitting the bottom.
But there's one other thing I remember, and remembering, I keep a grip on hope: GOD's loyal love couldn't have run out, his merciful love couldn't have dried up. They're created new every morning. How great your faithfulness! I'm sticking with GOD (I say it over and over). He's all I've got left. GOD proves to be good to the man who passionately waits, to the woman who diligently seeks. It's a good thing to quietly hope, quietly hope for help from GOD. ~ Lamentations 3:19-27 (MSG)

Praying you will go forth with a renewed hope knowing you are never alone...you are never helpless...because our Mighty God is with each and every one of us!

God bless!

Idella

189

ACKNOWLEDGMENTS

I am deeply indebted to my husband, Jack Edwards,
and daughter, Rhonda Andersen,
for their time and effort in proofing my book;
and to my family and friends
for their warm words of encouragement.

ABOUT THE AUTHOR

Born in 1940 and raised in Aurora, Illinois, Idella attended Olivet Nazarene University and received a degree from College of DuPage in Glen Ellyn, Illinois. She and her husband, Jack, have five children and twelve grandchildren and have lived in eight different states. They spent several years coordinating Lay Witness Missions and served as Certified Lay Speakers for the United Methodist Church for over 20 years.

Idella Edwards retired from the State of Oklahoma in 2005. She and her husband moved to Marion, Illinois where she is an active member of Aldersgate United Methodist Church. She writes a monthly faith column for The Marion Star Newspaper. She is a member of The Little Egypt Writers' Society in Marion and a board member of The Little Egypt Arts Association.

Previous publications include a poetry book, "MAGNIFY"; devotional books, "LOOK AT THE BIRDS", "DON'T HANG YOUR HARPS ON THE WILLOW TREE", and "ALL THINGS NEW"; and four children's books, "THE ADVENTURES OF TRUDY THE TREE SWALLOW", "I'M JUST DUCKY", "A VACATION TO REMEMBER" and "HAPPY TO BE ME."

In addition to spoiling the grandchildren, her favorite pastimes are jigsaw puzzles, writing poetry, bird watching, and photography.

DEAR GOD

Who is like You, Almighty God?
A greater god, there is none!
Yours, O Lord, is the greatness and the power,
Many are the wonders You have done!

Search me, O God, and know my heart
Forgive my foolish ways;
Set my feet on the solid rock
To serve You all my days.

Fill me with the knowledge of Your perfect will
In everything I do.
May the eyes of my heart be enlightened with hope
And my life pleasing to You.

~ Idella Pearl Edwards

CPSIA information can be obtained
at www.ICGtesting.com
Printed in the USA
FSHW010108040621
81961FS